Believing God's Perspective, Design, and Purpose for Women

A Six-Week Bible Study Based on Psalm 144:12

A "Shine" Book By Debbie M. Presnell

Name: Debbie M. Presnell
Title: Believing God's Perspective, Design, and Purpose for Women: A Six-Week Bible Study Based on Psalm 144:12

ISBN: 9798990083400
Library of Congress Control Number: 2024903887

Front cover credit: Maida Yaqoob from Fiverr, id: fiverr.com/design_maida

Published by
Shine Publishing
Black Mountain, North Carolina

What others are saying about *Believing God's Perspective, Design, and Purpose for Women*

In a world filled with conflicting messages about identity and purpose, "Believing God's Perspective, Design, and Purpose for Women" stands as a guiding light.

What sets this book apart is its genuine and compassionate tone. Debbie's enthusiasm for living for Christ shines through every page. Her depth of Biblical knowledge and profound insights offers a refreshing and encouraging perspective on what it means to be a woman in God's eyes and a deeper understanding of their unique role in God's grand design.

Debbie Presnell speaks directly to the hearts of women, offering insights that are both timely and timeless, making this book a valuable resource for women of all ages and walks of life.

Brad Simon
Author, *Encounters In Scripture* devotional and
featured Bible Teacher on Monday Morning Inspiration podcast.
Discover his Bible Teaching Ministry at: BWSimon.com

With sound biblical teaching and practical application, Debbie Presnell knows how to reach women where they are and lead them into a deeper relationship with God. Whether you're beginning your faith journey or you're a seasoned Bible student, Debbie will guide you into greater understanding and appreciation of God's Word in ways that will enable you to move toward a life-changing awareness of God's perspective, design, and purpose for women.

Denise K. Loock
Founder, DigDeeperDevotions.com
Author, *Open Your Hymnal: Devotions That Harmonize Scripture with Song*

Debbie Presnell shines everywhere she goes. Without even knowing her, you can tell she is a woman who loves Jesus. Despite a childhood where Satan tried to convince her otherwise, Debbie is an amazing woman whom God has called to encourage other women to seek God and make Him part of their lives.

Thank you, Debbie Presnell, for showing us all how to shine through life. You are a great example to show us God's Perspective, Design, and Purpose for Women.

Linda Gilden
Author, award winning editor, best-selling author,
writing and speaking coach, and
Director of the Carolina Christian Writers Conference
author of over 40 books and two thousand magazine articles

I dedicate this book to

Emma Danzy

You inspired me to dive deep into all aspects of Psalm 144:12 for its brilliant, life-changing meaning. After years of research, I came away with a true understanding of God's view and purpose for women. With new direction, I can share specific ways in which we can carry the light to others so they can shine too.
I also gained a forever friendship with you. I love you.

CONTENTS

View Why We Need This Study
Video on YouTube:

Hi friends! I am so grateful that you have chosen to study God's word with *Believing God's Perspective, Design, and Purpose for Women.* We need to explore the Bible together. Why? Well, a lot of reasons but here's just a couple. Many of us believe in God but doubt His words. Others believe what He says but tell themselves that God's words and promises are meant for others. How do we know this? Look around.

We recognize defeat on women's faces.

We hear fear and confusion in their conversations.

And many of these women are Christians desiring to follow God.

Now wait. I'm not talking about a bad day or crying sad tears. Crying is good for us, and a bad day is normal.

I'm talking about habitual defeat—a way of life. Satan's behind this. He schemes to break us—to shatter our true identity and render us ineffective. Because what we think, how we respond, and what we do, hinges on our identity.

Like many of you, I've been on the receiving end of Satan's attacks on my identity and self-worth. All of them were (and still are) vicious; some are subtle. Flashbacks make my heart race—for two reasons. First, sadness flows from identifying the deception that significantly shaped my thinking from childhood. Second, anger. Yep. Anger. Although I was a Christ-follower, I didn't have the knowledge, spiritual maturity, or tools to help me figure out what is truth and what is a lie.

Why is it easier to believe lies?

I wish I had fully understood the value, worth, and mission of a woman when I was younger. It's evident that millions of women of all ages are still trying to figure out her worth and role.

You may feel inadequate. In one way, there's no shame in that. Humility leads us to seek God's direction in whatever we do. This is especially true when we seek God's help to correct a faulty mindset or attitude.

A crisis in self-worth attacks our self-confidence squashing our joy and suppressing what could be a victorious, productive life. Often, we're stuck, wondering how we can fulfill our God-given purpose—those desires He placed within our heart. Maybe we don't mean to, but comparing ourselves to other women fuels this self-sabotaging mindset, a cycle the devil loves to wash over us, then spin, and repeat:

- You're not enough.
- You're less than.
- Your ideas are stupid.

For decades, women across the globe have heard the same speeches, debates, and protests. We've read thousands of articles and books. Yet we question our value and worth. Of course we do. There's a lot of conflicting information. Diverse philosophies, ideas, and experiences make womanhood a controversial topic. The book you're holding, however, is based on one perspective and plan—God's.

God's book, the Bible, contains life-altering principles to guide and help us better dispel the myths surrounding who we are in Christ. We can have God's truth right in front of us, and His empowering Holy Spirit living within us. How amazing! God has given us our senses to experience His truth first hand.

Hebrews 5:14 tells us, *[Our] senses [are]exercised to discern both good and evil.*

In this study you will engage your senses and be challenged to:
- *think* differently, more decisively, more consistently
- *see* yourself through another lens
- *say* what you wish you had known
- *feel* invigorated and enthusiastic
- *smell* the sweet aroma of a confirmed or validated identity in Christ
- *hear* God's loving voice
- *act* on new convictions

Expect to be influenced or touched uniquely. We cannot spend time in God's Word and not be different—in fact, transformed!

Together we'll do more than just believe in God. We'll *believe Him*. In John 14:10–11 Jesus said three times *Believe Me.*

As we read and study passages in God's Word, the wisdom we acquire will impact all areas of our daily life—physical, emotional, mental, spiritual, and relational.

When you finish this study, I pray you will emerge with a solid identity that propels you to live out your purpose in victory.

When we shine the light of God's truth, we break through the veil of darkness. Then, like a million flickering diamonds against a pitch-black backdrop, we shine.

Believing God's Perspective, Design, and Purpose for Women is a six-week study designed for individual or group study. An introduction jumpstarts each week, followed by five days of independent study. The sixth week, our conclusion, has only one lesson. Quoted scriptures primarily come from the New King James Version (NKJV); when another version is used, it's noted. Keep in mind as you study, when a Bible version uses small caps for the word LORD it signifies the Hebrew word *Yahweh,* the eternal *I Am* (from a root word meaning "to be," or eternal existence). When the word Lord is written with standard capitalization, it is personal, signifying the Hebrew word *Adonai,* literally meaning "my lord," (from a root word which suggests sovereignty, strength, and power).[1]

Additionally, the NKJV uses the word *man* in a generic sense; sometimes it refers to men and women and other times it's masculine specific. The meaning depends on whether the root is Hebrew or Greek. When God speaks to a people group and uses the word *man,* He is speaking to all mankind—all humans.

The time you spend in each chapter will vary. I encourage you to pray before beginning each study and ask God to reveal what He wants you to see and learn. Be honest with God and yourself. Let the journey begin. Let's shine together … forever!

The fact that I am a woman does not make me a different kind of Christian, but the fact that I am a Christian makes me a different kind of woman.

Elisabeth Elliot

<u>**Introduction: Week One—She's Strong**</u>

Participant's Guide

The study you're holding focuses on one source and one author,

____

and ___________________________________.

That our ___________________________________ _may be_

___________________________,

___________________________________ _in palace style._

The King James Version uses _______________________________ and

_____________________.

The New International Version uses _____________________________ and

_____________________.

The New American Standard Version uses _____________________ and

_____________________.

According to Psalm 144:12, godly women are:

____

____

____

____

____

Introduction: Week One—She's Strong

View Introduction:
Week One Video on YouTube:

Hello friends! I'm so excited to go on this journey with you for the next six weeks—a journey to know and believe God's perspective, design, and purpose for women.

Whether we're young or older or somewhere in the middle, we've all been exposed to various opinions and ideas about women. You know—their role, worth, and purpose.

Some women view themselves as so strong and capable, that they're working twenty-five-hours a day, feeling underappreciated, overwhelmed, and worn out. A clear vision or boundary line, marking where something starts or ends, is blurred.

Do you sometimes want to exchange your Superwoman cape for a lounge chair on the beach or a hammock in the mountains?

Me, too.

Perhaps you're on the opposite end of the spectrum. Your peers in school (elementary, middle, and high school) or the adults in your life beat you down with verbal insults.

You've heard, "You can't get anything right, You'll never be good enough. Your ideas are stupid."

Your self-worth languishes in the muddy trenches. You find it difficult to recognize your talents and abilities. And if you did identify them, you'd bury them in the trench beside your self-worth, because in your mind others are more capable. You feel stuck. Noticing others' achievements on social media stirs up the sludge in your dark, drizzling season.

Maybe you're somewhere in the middle. Or perhaps you're in a good place and you want to keep the momentum. I hear you.

No matter the season of life we're in, everything we think or do hinges on our identity in Christ and what we believe about Him.

When I was nine years old, I loved Jesus and wanted Him to lead my life, so I became a Christ-follower. With Jesus leading, I developed new thought patterns. When I walked home from school, for example, I prayed and asked Jesus to protect me from the neighborhood dogs and to take away my fear of them. I learned early He would help me.

Two years later, my parents divorced. In the 1970s, divorce wasn't as common or as accepted as it is now. When my mom, brothers, and I moved in the middle of my sixth-grade school year from the West Coast to the East Coast, the devil told me I was different—the only one from a broken family and I would never be accepted. A new mentality surfaced:

My earthly father left because I wasn't worth keeping.

Although my peers in my new school never treated me badly (or at least badly enough to remember), I was still too spiritually immature to quiet the negative voice in my head. But after years of regular church attendance, I established friendships within my youth group, and my attitude changed. I learned sign language and became one of the interpreters for the deaf in my church. Now, I was special.

But Satan didn't retreat. Fast-forward to my senior year of high school. My friends were headed to college. My family was too poor to afford a college education, especially a private Christian education. The devil shouted, "You haven't done well enough in school to qualify for an academic scholarship." He planted within me the notion I would be left behind—never able to achieve my dreams. I wallowed in self-pity.

I'm not good enough; I don't have what it takes.

I continued to pray the only way I knew how—simply and transparently. *Help me* was still my best prayer.

My heavenly Father picked me up because I was worthy, and He had a plan.

A month later, a private Christian university contacted me and asked if I would become a deaf interpreter for their school. The payment? A full four-year scholarship. Yes, I was learning to trust God.

I graduated at the age of twenty-one, started my teaching career, married the love of my life, and then started graduate school.

As I grew in my relationship with Christ, Satan continued to attack my self-worth. I was delighted to be offered a faculty position at a local college until the devil cleverly (and falsely) persuaded me I secured the job only because no one else had applied. His attack was methodical and convincing. I was defenseless, or so I thought. I couldn't accept that I was worthy. Disappointment eclipsed my joy.

And so it continued. Decade after decade, in every challenge or blessing, Satan screamed the same lies.

Here's hope.

Satan knows when we gaze on Jesus, we become stronger, wiser, and better able to identify his harmful attacks, then counter them with God's truth. Confusion and pain in the dark space is replaced by the God's warmth and light.

In his letter to the church in Rome, Paul writes, *For they exchanged the truth of God for falsehoods* (Romans 1:25). Do you know the truth?

It can be confusing because so much has been written about women. The viewpoints expressed by various authors are as diverse as the women who read them—different theories, philosophies, and theologies. And because these viewpoints are often contradictory, what we choose to believe depends on our individual experiences, the people who have had a significant impact in our lives, and the strength we must have to believe that which is true. John 8:32 tells us, *The truth will see you free.* Now that's freedom.

The study you're holding focuses on one source and one author—the Bible and Almighty God. Although we will study dozens of scriptures in the Bible, the premise is the second half of Psalm 144:12, which reads in the New King James Version:

> *That our daughters may be as pillars, sculptured in palace style.*

The New King James Version uses *pillars* and *sculptured*. But check out the similar verbiage in these translations:

The King James Version is the only translation to use the words *polished* and *cornerstones*.

The New International Version uses *pillars* and *carved to adorn*.

The New American Standard Bible uses *pillars* and *fashioned*.

Wanting to get a better understanding of the word "polished" in this context I looked up the word in the *Merriam-Webster's Dictionary* and found that polished means "shiny, a result of being rubbed." As a noun polished means "a high state of development or refinement." As a verb, it means, "to make smooth" which is what it means in Hebrew too.[2]

Bible commentator Matthew Henry wrote:

> "When women are adorned with the graces of God's Spirit, which are the polishing of that which is naturally rough, and 'become women professing godliness' and purified and consecrated to God as living temples, they are polished after the similitude of the palace."[3]

To further help me grasp this verse I researched the word *Cornerstone* and learned it is defined as, "something of basic importance; a basic element—the foundation."[4]

In the context of Psalm 144:12, biblical scholars liken a polished woman to an ornamental column of a palace, chiseled by a sculptor.

Comparing a woman to a pillar may not be the object we'd compare ourselves to. We'd rather picture a woman's beauty and strength as a resilient flower bud piercing through the snow-covered ground and blossoming, or as a determined caterpillar that transforms into a colorful butterfly.

But when we dive deeper and discover the intended purpose of a column, the symbolisms are inspiring.

I mean, take a look at ancient ruins. What's left standing? In the midst of the rubble, stands a pillar. Yeah.

A pillar, or palace column, is weight-bearing, supportable, and dependable. Some of the current architectural columns still standing in Athens, Greece, were constructed when the apostle Paul was preaching. Again, intriguing support and visual evidence of why God chose *pillar* to describe a godly woman. She is a strong foundation with lasting influence, even thousands of years.

Just as columns support the structure, godly women nurture, undergird, and lift one another. Their God-given strength gives them the capacity to resist Satan's lies and embrace truth.

As we continue to study Psalm 144:12, we'll discover God's view of women.

In Week One, we'll see that women are strong. They have the capacity, strength, and boldness to embrace their true identity and deny what's false.

In Week Two, we'll learn the depth of a woman's beauty. Made in God's image makes us beautiful because He is beautiful. The Bible tells us in Psalm 34:5, *Those who look to him are radiant* (NIV). Girl, you can shine! Your undeniable glow lights up a room.

In Week Three, we'll examine true wisdom. This godly wisdom enables a woman to build a home, community, and nation.

In Week Four, we'll study what it means for a woman to be polished in the refining fires that purify her character.

In Week Five, we'll inspect what it means to be likened to a pillar and cornerstone, women who are positioned to nurture, uphold, and leave a lasting legacy.[5]

We'll wrap up in Week Six with "Your Story: Shining the Light for Greatest Impact."

God created women. He knows our worth, value, and abilities. God enabled numerous women in the Bible to accomplish His plan. During our six-week study, we'll talk about Esther, Puah, Shiphuah, Jochebed, Abigail, Priscilla, Rahab, Mary of Bethany, Martha, Mary (mother of Jesus), and Hannah.

Let's talk about one of them right now—Esther. While a portion of her story unfolded like a modern-day reality television show, Esther exhibited dignity, strength, humility, compassion, selflessness, courage, discernment, wisdom, and power under control. She used both her external and internal beauty to glorify God and accomplish His will. Her story is told in ten chapters in the book of Esther. Here's a summary:

> Esther, a Jewish orphan, was raised by her cousin Mordecai. When she was a teenager, she was chosen to appear before the king in a beauty contest. The winner would become queen. Fearing prejudice might prevent her from becoming queen, Esther kept her Jewish heritage a secret. For the next year, she took part in beauty treatments—six months of oils and six more months of fragrant spices—while she waited her turn to go before the king. When Esther went before King Ahasuerus (King Xerxes), she found favor with him, and he crowned her queen.
>
> Later, a man named Haman, rose to such power that officials knelt before him to show respect. But Mordecai refused to bow to anyone except God, and that infuriated Haman. Haman knew Mordecai was a Jew, so he conspired to kill every Jew in the kingdom. Mordecai asked Esther to use her influence as queen and beg the king for mercy for the Jewish people. Esther had a choice—be scared or be obedient. Because the day of death for the Jews was still eleven months away, she could have waited. But Mordecai said she had become queen for such a time as this (Esther 4:14). In other words, don't procrastinate. Esther approached the king and asked him to spare her life and her people's lives. The king was outraged when he heard about Haman's plot. So, Haman was hanged, and Esther destroyed a wicked conspiracy to kill all the Jews in the Persian Empire.[6]

We'll read more about the details this week on Day 4. But for now, do you know the significance of her name? Esther's Hebrew name was Hadassah which means myrtle or set on a high place. And Esther means "star." Positioned in a high place, Esther humbled herself to seek after God and obey His will.

A shining star indeed!

Esther may have been orphaned when her parents died, but she wasn't orphaned by God. He took what appeared to be misfortunes and turned them into divine appointments, using each one as a link in the chain of good things to come.

We can be a modern-day Esther. Our God-given strength enables us to believe and take action.

Over the course of this first week, we'll talk about strength:

Day 1: Strength to Embrace Her True Identity, Part 1

Day 2: Strength to Embrace Her True Identity, Part 2

Day 3: Strength to Resist the Enemy's Lies

Day 4: Strength to Live Courageously

Day 5: Strength to Stand in Righteousness

Before we go any further, memorize Philippians 4:13: *I can do all things through Christ who strengthens me.* Because Christ lives in us (Galatians 2:20), we can relinquish our thoughts of living independently. We were created to rely on Him. His strength, not our own, enables us to act courageously and to boldly believe and embrace God's perspective of a godly woman.

Week One, Day 1

Strength to Embrace Her True Identity ~ Part 1

*I will love You, O LORD, my strength. The LORD is my rock and my fortress and
my deliverer; my God, my strength, in whom I will trust; my shield and the horn
of my salvation, my stronghold.*

Psalm 18:1–2

Pivotal Point: God gives us strength to believe Him.

When I was a teenager, I bravely carried my Bible to school. My mom, pastors,
and Sunday school teachers taught me about God, so I had a reservoir of head
knowledge. And I loved Jesus, so I wanted to please Him. But my head and heart
weren't in sync. Comparing myself to others dulled my light, specifically the
shining Light of Jesus, to whom I had surrendered:

I wasn't enough—beautiful enough, smart enough, strong enough.

Perhaps your spiritual foundation is similar to mine. Maybe, though, you weren't
raised with specific convictions, and biblical concepts are foreign to you—
especially God's view of you.

Technology and social media have made it easier to compare ourselves to the
world's beliefs, making us question what we accept as truth or how we measure
up.

Most of us have heard God exists, loves this vast world, and sent His Son as a
sacrifice to save it. But do you secretly wonder if God loves *you*?

Childhood memories and traumatic events can impact our self-worth and our view
of God. Sometimes we equate unworthiness in the eyes of others as unworthiness
in the eyes of God. Our feelings may be justified, but they are also skewed.

Why do we think this way? Author Priscilla Shirer answers the question:

> That's what the enemy wants. He wants you living in a state of
> defeat. Your defenses down. Your resolve weak and flimsy.
> Surrendering to an army of insecurities and misdiagnosis instead of
> courageously thriving in the sophisticated security of your identity
> in Christ.[8]

"Courageously thriving." Hmm, never thought about the courage required to really believe.

Reflect on any defining memories or highpoints from your childhood. In what way do they contribute to how you view God and how you think He sees you?

Sometimes how we view ourselves is also how we think God sees us. How do you see yourself today? If you were describing yourself in the third person, what would you say about yourself? Be completely transparent and circle all that apply.

Insignificant	Worthy	Special
Cherished	Messed Up	Forgotten
Useful	Worthless	Judged
Invisible	Unlovable	Hopeless
Prideful	Guilty	Shameful
Hesitant	Afraid	Stuck
Other ___________		

How does your description of yourself compare to how God sees you? (Not how you know you *should* feel, but the deep truth before God.)

Maybe you're unsure right now. It's okay. We'll come back to your description later.

The Bible tells us the truth about the way God views us. Ask Him right now to give you the strength to believe and the confidence to live into your identity as His child.

Let's take off on this wild, wonderful journey and start at the very beginning.

Read Genesis 1:26–27:

> *Then God said, "Let Us make man in Our image, according to Our likeness; let them have dominion over the fish of the sea, over the birds of the air, and over the cattle, over all the earth and over every creeping thing that creeps on the earth." So God created man in His own image; in the image of God He created him; male and female He created them.*

It should be enough that God says we're made by Him and in His image. But in a sin-infested, flesh-driven world, it's not always believable. We listen to what others say because we think their opinions matter. Stop for moment and breathe in this truth from God:

> I'm made in the image of Almighty God. The beauty in the world testifies to His beauty. Therefore, I am beautiful.

Oh, the truth gets even sweeter. For music lovers of a certain age, you may recall when Stevie Wonder released the song, "You Are the Sunshine of My Life." In the lyrics, he used a phrase from Scripture, "You are the apple of my eye."

God first used this expression in the Old Testament to show He cares for His people: *He found him in a desert land and in the wasteland, a howling wilderness; He encircled him, He instructed him, He kept him as the apple of His eye* (Deuteronomy 32:10).

The phrase "apple of my eye" means we're cherished. The apple, or pupil, is considered the most delicate part of the eye. When we look into another person's eyes, we see our reflection. Similarly, when God looks into our eyes, He sees His reflection.

The psalmist understood how God felt about him when he wrote Psalm 17:8: *Keep me as the apple of your eye; hide me under the shadow of Your wings. Oh, how cherished we are!*

Perhaps right now you're thinking, Hang on a minute. Maybe you slowly shook your head and said, Not me. I'm too sinful for God to see Himself in me. After all, He is Holy. And you are right—God is holy and none of us are worthy to stand before a holy God. Romans 3:10 confirms we are sinners: *There is none righteous, no, not one.*

But because God loves us so much, He provided atonement for our sin. Atonement is defined as a "making up for an offense or injury; satisfaction; the reconciliation of God and humankind through the sacrificial death of Jesus Christ."[9]

Go to 1 John 4:9–10 and see this for yourself. Who made atonement for us? Why was atonement necessary? Who paid the price?

Read 1 Corinthians 6:20 and summarize what it says.

Flip back to Romans 9:25 and fill in the blank. God says He makes us His _____________________________. And to the unloved, He makes them _____________________________.

As His beloved, God's affection gets more personal. He:

- Knows our name (Isaiah 43:1)
- Knows the number of hairs on our head (Luke 12:7)
- Tells us to call on Him (Jeremiah 33:3)
- Desires we let Him take our worries (1 Peter 5:7)
- Tells us how to live an incredibly good life (Proverbs 7:2)
- Wants us to call Him Father (Jeremiah 3:19)

Being beloved by God is a life-changing epiphany.

This next passage is mind-blowing. Read Psalm 139:17–18 and fill in the missing words:

How precious also are Your thoughts to _____________________________, O God! How great is the sum of them! If I should count them, they would be more in number than the _____________________________; when I awake, I am still with You.

Scientist Robert Krulwich writes, "If you assume a grain of sand has an average size, and you calculate how many grains are in a teaspoon and then multiply by all the beaches and deserts in the world, the Earth has roughly (and we're speaking very roughly here) 7.5 x 10^{18} grains of sand, or seven quintillion, five hundred quadrillion grains."[10]

I can't even write those numbers.

It's unfathomable.

God's thoughts about us outnumber the grains of sand. He never takes a break from thinking about us and what concerns us.

Do you believe God cares about you? Do you believe you're always on His mind? If yes, how does this understanding affect your mindset throughout the day? If no, what is the hardest part about believing?

God's truth gets better and better. Read Ephesians 2:10. What claim does God make about you?

Depending on your Bible translation, you may have answered *handiwork, masterpiece,* or *workmanship*. What does workmanship mean to you? How does it specifically apply to you?

God—Creator of the universe—calls us His masterpiece and a finished product. Scrolling through social media could make us feel less-than, insignificant, or unworthy. So, before you scroll, write, "God said I'm His masterpiece" on a sticky note and place it on your computer or phone. In fact, attach this phrase and verse everywhere!

Wow. We've only opened the door to God's truth a little bit, but already the sunshine is coming through, casting a beam of light on the path in front of us. Tomorrow, in "Strength to Embrace Her Identity ~ Part 2," we'll swing the door wide open.

What specifically are you choosing to believe from God's Word today?

Day One's Sparkling Gem: I believe I am divinely created, cherished, perfectly designed, capable, and useful for God's purpose.

Prayer: Father, help me believe You love me regardless of my mistakes and You will never remove Your love from me. Strengthen me to believe You care about the important things in my life and minute details too. Help me remember whose I am and I am who I am because of You. In Jesus's name, amen.

Perspective: On a piece of paper, write down the alphabet from A–Z. Beside each letter, write something that is true of the believer in Christ. For example, A = Apple of His eye, B = Beloved, C = Cared for, and so on. If you are unsure, ask a friend to help you.

Week One, Day 2

Strength to Embrace Her True Identity ~ Part 2

It is not my ability, but my response to God's ability, that counts.
Corrie Ten Boom[11]

Behold what manner of love the Father has bestowed on us, that we should be called children of God! Therefore the world does not know us, because it did not know Him. Beloved, now we are children of God; and it has not yet been revealed what we shall be, but we know that when He is revealed, we shall be like Him, for we shall see Him as He is. And everyone who has this hope in Him purifies himself, just as He is pure.

1 John 3:1–3

Pivotal Point: God gives us access to supernatural strength.

DNA testing has become popular in recent years. No surprise there. People want to know their ancestry. As Christ-followers, however, we have more than earthly relatives who pass down qualities, characteristics, and distinct mannerisms. We belong to God, and this truth changes everything. He is our Father, and we can have His character. Oh, girl, this is great news!

Romans 8:12–17 tells us:

> *Therefore, brethren, we are debtors—not to the flesh, to live according to the flesh. For if you live according to the flesh you will die; but if by the Spirit you put to death the deeds of the body, you will live. For as many as are led by the Spirit of God, these are sons of God. For you did not receive the spirit of bondage again to fear, but you received the Spirit of adoption by whom we cry out, "Abba, Father." The Spirit Himself bears witness with our spirit that we are children of God, and if children, then heirs—heirs of God and joint heirs with Christ, if indeed we suffer with Him, that we may also be glorified together.*

Right! When we believe Jesus is the Son of God, He died for our sins and rose again, and we trust Him as our Savior, we're adopted into God's family. We weren't worthy on our own or accepted because of our good works. Being created in God's image is what gives us worth. God saw we were worth dying for. We're His children.

The word *adoption* comes from the Latin word *adoptare,* meaning "taken by choice."[12] God chose us to be part of His royal family. What does adoption by God mean to you?

Match the following verses to their reference. The word *son* is used to represent mankind. These verses describe your new identity:

____ Galatians 3:26

A. *Therefore you are no longer a slave but a son, and if a son, then an heir of God through Christ.*

____ Galatians 4:7

B. *Now, therefore, you are no longer strangers and foreigners, but fellow citizens with the saints and members of the household of God.*

____ Ephesians 2:19

C. *I will be a Father to you, and you shall be My sons and daughters, says the LORD Almighty.*

____ 2 Corinthians 6:18

D. *You are all sons of God through faith in Christ Jesus.*

Read John 1:12. What do we gain when we receive Jesus Christ?

Our earthly fathers may be absent emotionally or physically, but our heavenly Father will never abandon us. He provides, protects, values, and cherishes. He models love, loyalty, forgiveness, and discipline. Although earthly fathers make mistakes, God never does.

God is the perfect Father.

When adopted as His child, we're simultaneously sealed and set apart. To help us better understand this significance, let's look back in history.

In many cultures, a king's package or letter was stamped with a seal to show its authenticity. If the package lacked the seal, it was considered inauthentic. The royal seal on a package also indicated its great worth, because it belonged to the king. When we choose to put our faith in Jesus Christ, Ephesians 1:13 tells us, *Having believed, you were sealed with the Holy Spirit of promise.*

God sets His seal on us; we're sealed as children of God and sealed by the Holy Spirit. We belong to Him; our eternal security is guaranteed. God is the King of kings, and we are authentically His. Now we're a beautiful package.

In what way will believing you're stamped with God's seal of approval change how you react when others disapprove of you?

Read Psalm 4:3 and fill in the missing word:

But know that the LORD has _______________________________ for Himself him who is godly; the LORD will hear when I call to Him.

Because we are adopted and bear God's seal, we're also set apart to obey His commandments. We obey His commandments because we love Him. In doing so, we position ourselves for blessing.

Additionally, to be set apart is to be saved or used for a particular purpose. In this way, we're set apart to shine His love and point others to Him. We'll be different. We won't love what this world loves, and we won't value what the world values.

We are God's daughters, and Philippians 2:15 tells us, *Live clean, innocent lives as children of God, shining like bright lights in a world full of crooked and perverse people* (NLT).

The world needs our light—even if people don't realize that. We're able to shine the light because God's Spirit resides within us. Keep on: *Let your light so shine*

before men, that they may see your good works and glorify your Father in heaven
(Matthew 5:16).

What is one way you are set apart and shining like a bright light in your
workplace? If you're not, how can you shine more brightly?

In your home?

And in your community?

Throughout this chapter, we've seen what happens when we become Christ-
followers. God made humanity, but not all humans acknowledge or accept this
truth. Not all humans choose to become His children. If you haven't been adopted
into His family yet, this is where your new identity begins. Go to Appendix A to
learn how you can place your faith in Jesus Christ.

Let's conclude by personalizing God's intentional, powerful, and life-changing
message. Print your name in the blanks.

The Lord appeared to him from afar, saying, *I have loved*
[________________], with an everlasting love; therefore, I have drawn you
with lovingkindness. Jeremiah 31:3 (NASB)

God so loved [________________________], that He gave His only
begotten Son, that if [________________________] believes in Him
[________________]should not perish, but have everlasting life. John 3:16

You created my inner most parts; You wove [________________] in my
mother's womb. I [____________] will give thanks to You, for I [________]

am awesomely and wonderfully made; wonderful are Your works, and my soul knows it very well. Psalm 139:13–14 (NASB)

The LORD your God in your midst, the Mighty One, will save; He will rejoice over you [________________________________] with gladness, He will quiet [________________] with His love, He will rejoice over [____________________________] with singing. Zephaniah 3:17

Our actions, responses, and attitudes reflect what we believe about God, our identity in Him, and His purpose for us. With these truths burned into our heart, we'll confidently light up any room.

What specifically are you choosing to believe from God's Word today?

Day Two's Sparkling Gem: I believe I am an adopted daughter of the King of kings, am sealed and set apart for Him, and the recipient of supernatural strength.

Prayer: Oh Father, give me daily wisdom to discern what is true and what is a lie. Strengthen my mind and heart. Help me believe the truth of my identity in You. In Jesus's name, amen.

Perspective: Which verses from Day One and Day Two had the greatest impact on you? Write these on sticky notes or note cards. Attach these notes to your bathroom vanity mirror, on the refrigerator, near the coffeemaker, or any place you frequently look. Start your day with the truth of God.

Strength to Resist the Enemy's Lies

*We're going to have to let truth scream louder to our souls
than the lies that have infected us.*
Beth Moore[13]

Yours, O LORD, is the greatness, the power and the glory, the victory and the majesty; for all that is in heaven and in earth is Yours; Yours is the kingdom, O LORD, and You are exalted as head over all. Both riches and honor come from You, and You reign over all. In Your hand is power and might; in Your hand it is to make great and to give strength to all. Now therefore, our God, we thank You and praise Your glorious name.
1 Chronicles 29:11–13

Pivotal Point: God gives us strength to resist deception.

Written in the preface of *The Screwtape Letters*, author C.S. Lewis gives this advice:

"Readers are advised to remember: the devil is a liar."

Merriam-Webster's Dictionary defines *liar* as "one who tells lies."[14] Yep. Summed up perfectly. Everything the devil says is a lie. He is a deceiver, fraudster, swindler, imposter, and fabricator. He's the ultimate adversary—mine, yours, and God's.

Do you have other names for the devil? How does John 8:44 identify him?

And if being a deceiver isn't bad enough, there's more. Read John 10:10. What three things does the thief—the devil—come to do?

In the following section, you'll read about six women from the Bible who fell captive to the Deceiver's lies. From our vantage point as women, it may be easier to imagine the lies or the perceived lies these women struggled with.

Eve lived in paradise. She had never experienced rejection, envy, guilt, disorder, grief, embarrassment, pain, or confusion of any sort until she listened to the Enemy. Read Genesis 3:1–7. What was the lie?

Hagar, an Egyptian slave, who became one of Abraham's wives and Sarah's rival, escaped to the wilderness in desperation. Read Genesis 16:1–16. What lies could Satan have filled her head with?

The Widow, who was extremely poor gave two mites. The Greek word for mites is *lepta* and means two copper coins worth less than a penny.[15] Read Mark 12:41–44. What possible lies could the devil have declared prior to her act of generosity?

The Woman with the Issue of Blood suffered a chronic illness, which made her a social outcast. Read Matthew 9:20–22. What are the plausible fabrications the Enemy told her during her twelve years of sickness?

The Sinful Woman sought repentance from Jesus. She ignored the stares of the men and approached Jesus with an alabaster jar of expensive perfume. She poured the precious perfume on Jesus's feet and wiped them with her hair. Read Luke 7:36–50. In what ways might Satan have attacked her mind?

Martha was a close friend of Jesus. When her brother Lazarus died and Jesus didn't come in the expected time frame, Martha reacted in frustration. Read John 11:1–46. What lies do you think Satan tormented her with?

This same Martha had an episode of anger and indignation while cleaning her house and preparing food to serve Jesus. Read Luke 10:38–42. In what ways did Satan rile her up?

Look at the following list. Did any of your answers resemble these?

- You're confused.
- God didn't really say that.
- Your gift is too small to be useful.
- God doesn't need your money.
- Others offer better gifts.
- No one cares about you.
- You're wasting your time.
- Everyone will judge you.
- You're not worthy or good enough.
- Your sin is too great.
- Observers will call you a hypocrite.
- You have an embarrassing past.

- You'll never be forgiven.
- Jesus won't accept you.
- Jesus forgot about you.
- Jesus isn't dependable.
- God doesn't care about you.
- Stay busy.
- You aren't appreciated.
- You're shameful.

All lies.

Which of the lies listed above are you currently struggling with? Circle all that apply. If none of these lies apply, is there another? If not, what do you do to resist the devil's lies?

What lie, if any, is easier to believe than others?

In modern times, Satan has added new weapons to his arsenal: social media, television, and secular magazines. You know the magazines—the ones suggesting we should look a certain way or be a specific size. They imply we're not enough. The devil also uses television and social media to persuade us that a compromise in our values will bring ultimate satisfaction and that fulfillment and happiness can be found in self-indulgence, success, and good times.

Satan's agenda is always the same: slither into our lives, kill our passions and dreams, steal our peace and joy, and destroy our witness and relationships.

None of us are immune to Satan's tactics. We battle right and wrong, truth and lies. Sometimes a fierce fight develops in our head. But we can rise above the devil's schemes and be victorious.

Ephesians 6:11 shows us how to successfully fight the battle raging in our mind: *Put on the full armor of God, so that you will be able to stand firm against the schemes of the devil* (NASB).

Let's now turn to Ephesians 6:14–17 and describe the pieces of armor.

Gird yourself with ____.

The truth of God's Word holds us together. When Satan tempted Jesus, Jesus spoke the Scriptures to combat Satan's lies (Matthew 4:1–11). We can't fight with a weapon we don't have. We protect our minds when we fill it with God's truth, the truth found in God's Word.

When do you schedule Bible reading and prayer into your busy day?

Put on the breastplate of ________________________________.

A Roman soldier wore a breastplate in battle to protect his heart, lungs, and other vital organs. Paul used this analogy of a breastplate of righteousness because Jesus purchased our righteousness on the cross. At salvation, we're given the breastplate of righteousness to protect our heart and soul from Satan's evil attacks and deception. Our righteousness doesn't save us; Jesus's does. Therefore, we seek Him and delight in His commands.

What do you do to protect your heart? If unsure, what could you do better to protect your heart?

Cover your feet with the preparation of the ________________________.

When Satan attacks, we need to be vigilant and ready to go in another direction.

When I was a young woman beginning my career as a teacher, I learned the teachers' lounge sometimes became a place of gossip. I had to be intentional about staying away or going in the other direction.

Is there anything you need to walk away from? If so, what?

Take up the shield of _________________________________.

Our faith acts as a shield to deflect the flaming arrows of the devil. Hebrews 11:6 tells us, *Without faith it is impossible to please God.* When we're attacked, faith exhorts us to trust God. Faith helps us resist temptation. Faith reminds us of God's love.

What, if anything, causes you to doubt God's plan or His for you?

Wear the helmet of _________________________________.

When my husband rode his motorcycle on a beautiful day, he wore the necessary protective gear: boots, a jacket with armored plates, leather pants or long jeans, and gloves. He put on the most important protection last—his helmet. Soldiers and motorcycle riders need a helmet to protect the brain. Spiritually speaking, the helmet protects our thoughts.

The assurance of our salvation is our defense against anything Satan throws at us. Psalm 140:7 tells us, *O GOD the Lord, the strength of my salvation, You have covered my head in the day of battle.*

What steps do you take to protect your mind?

Use the sword of the _________________________________.

The sword is an offensive weapon. God's Word is the sword we use to repel Satan's lies. Hebrews 4:12 tells us, *For the word of God is living and powerful, and sharper than any two-edged sword, piercing even to the division of soul and spirit, and of joints and marrow, and is a discerner of the thoughts and intents of the heart.*

Is part of your spiritual wardrobe missing? If so, which item?

Here's more good news!

John 16:13 tells us this: *However, when He, the Spirit of truth, has come, He will guide you into all truth; for He will not speak on His own authority, but whatever He hears He will speak; and He will tell you things to come.*

In the previous verse above, underline what the Holy Spirit—the Spirit of truth— guides us in.

The Holy Spirit exposes deceit and wrong motives; He helps us deny the lie.

Now read Psalm 119:18 written here: *Open my eyes, that I may see wondrous things from Your law.*

How does opening our spiritual eyes help us deny the lie?

With eyes wide open, we discover godly women are highly favored and strong. We can embrace the truth of who we are and refute the lies of the Enemy. With this amazing mindset, we will surely shine. As evangelist Dwight L. Moody said, "We are told to let our light shine, and if it does, we won't need to tell anybody it does. Lighthouses don't fire cannons to call attention to their shining—they just shine." [16]

What specifically are you choosing to believe from God's Word today?

Day Three's Sparkling Gem: I believe God provides me with strength to refute the devil's lies.

Prayer: Sovereign God, thank You for the strength to resist Satan's attacks. Open my eyes today to see what You want me to see. I am strong because the Holy Spirit lives within me and guides me into all truth. In Jesus's name, amen.

Perspective: The devil is after our children too. Teach a child how to fight his attacks by using the armor of God. Create homemade garments to demonstrate the armor and role play.

Week One, Day 4

Strength to Live Courageously

Deny your weakness, and you will never realize God's strength in you.
Joni Eareckson Tada[17]

Be strong and of good courage, do not fear nor be afraid of them; for the LORD your God, He is the One who goes with you. He will not leave you nor forsake you. Then Moses called Joshua and said to him in the sight of all Israel, "Be strong and of good courage, for you must go with this people to the land which the LORD has sworn to their fathers to give them, and you shall cause them to inherit it. And the LORD, He is the One who goes before you. He will be with you, He will not leave you nor forsake you; do not fear nor be dismayed."
Deuteronomy 31:6–8

Pivotal Point: God gives us courage in every season and circumstance.

It's been said Thomas Edison was afraid of the dark.[18] Does that surprise you? His fear propelled him to discover a way we could live in the light. His fear didn't suppress him—he courageously pushed through it, and his discovery of the light bulb changed the world.

We've all experienced fear at one time or another. The people in the Bible serve as our examples for overcoming fear and becoming courageous.

Two Courageous Midwives

We talked about Esther in this study's introduction. But centuries before Esther was placed in the palace and prepared for her role in saving the lives of the Jewish Nation, two other women also played a significant part in God's plan to rescue His people.

Puah and Shiphuah were midwives who boldly refused to obey Pharaoh's command to kill the male Hebrew babies at birth. Exodus 1:17 tells us these women feared God. These women were quick-witted too. When Pharaoh questioned them, what was their response? (Exodus 1:19)

Snicker. Why, those Hebrew women are lively!

Their faith compelled them to obey God. Without knowing what would be to come, they courageously put in motion God's miraculous plan. Move forward to the next chapter.

One Courageous Birth Mother

Jochebed was her name.

She was Moses's birth mother.

Exodus 2:2 tells us, *So the woman conceived and bore a son. And when she saw that he was a beautiful child, she hid him three months.*

Jochebed had a beautiful baby boy—and a problem.

> How can I save my son?

God impresses on her a divine plan.

> Wait. What? Put my baby in a basket and float him in the Nile? Aren't there crocodiles in there?

Scripture doesn't tell what was going through Jochebed's mind. What do you imagine are her fears and struggles? Did she pace the floor? Did she cry?

Despite hormones, sleep deprivation, fears, or questions, Exodus 2:3–4 says Jochebed obeyed God:

> *But when she could no longer hide him, she took an ark of bulrushes for him, daubed it with asphalt and pitch, put the child in it, and laid it in the reeds by the river's bank. And his sister stood afar off, to know what would be done to him.*

From where did she draw her strength?

It's likely Jochebed knew God intimately through spending time with Him in prayer. Perhaps she'd experienced His faithfulness in the past, and believed He could be trusted now—in this mysterious moment. Maybe all she could have known were stories of her ancestors.

Two midwives and one precious mother—set God's plan in motion. Moses grew in strength, character, knowledge, and wisdom, and eighty years later he led God's people out of bondage.

One Courageous Queen

Fast-forward a few centuries. Read Esther chapter four, then answer the following questions.

What did Esther tell Hathach (Hatach in KJV, Hathak in NIV) to tell Mordecai? (v. 11)

The law at this time prohibited anyone from approaching the king unless they were called or summoned. The consequence was death, unless the king held out his golden scepter to the person. This decree applied to all people—including the king's wife.

How long had it been since the king had summoned Esther? (v. 11)

What did Mordecai warn Esther about? (vv. 13–14)

What emotion(s) do you think surged within Esther?

What confidence did Mordecai give her?

What did Esther pledge to do for three days? (v. 16)

The dictionary defines *fasting* simply: "to abstain from food."[19]

But in a spiritual context, fasting is defined "as a way to show repentance and deny oneself the comforts of life, instead relying on God alone for strength."[20]

In the Bible, fasting means a person replaces eating with one or more of the following:

- Penitence (sorrow)
- Weeping
- Mourning (grieving)
- Petition (request, beg, plea)[21]

The disciples once asked Jesus why they could not cast a demon out of a man's son. Read His answer in Matthew 17:20–21:

> So Jesus said to them, "Because of your unbelief; for assuredly, I say to you, if you have faith as a mustard seed, you will say to this mountain, 'Move from here to there,' and it will move; and nothing will be impossible for you. However, this kind does not go out except by prayer and fasting."

With what did Jesus associate fasting?

Again, in Acts 13:2–3, Luke associates fasting with prayer:

> *As they ministered to the Lord and fasted, the Holy Spirit said,
> "Now separate to Me Barnabas and Saul for the work to which I
> have called them." Then, having fasted and prayed, and laid hands
> on them, they sent them away.*

What did Esther resolve to do? (v. 16)

Finally, Esther says, "And if I perish, I perish!"

Esther's courage came from God, as He answered her prayer, Mordecai's prayer,
and all the Jews praying in Shushan.

Two Midwives, One Mother, One Queen, and You

Satan uses fear to destroy the confidence God gives us to pursue our dreams,
passions, and purpose. When fear arises, God wants us to come to Him. He wants
to replace our fear with courage. This boldness allows us to push forward and
conquer something unknown or pull back and overcome a hindrance.

Perhaps you're facing a fearful situation. You need courage to:

- Begin a new ministry or job
- Accept your adult child is moving away
- Step away from a false security
- Stand up for a friend or an injustice
- Write a report, response, or rebuttal
- Face an unknown future

Can you relate to any of these? What do you need courage for in this season of
your life?

Sometimes the transition between our current situation—which may feel calm—and a new opportunity may feel risky or uncomfortable. The fear accompanying these emotions can be stifling, preventing us from moving forward in God's will. Procrastination and intimidation will not propel us into God's plan. Neither will dreaming, wishing, or hoping. Fear prevents us from succeeding in God's plans. We need courage to act.

God encouraged Joshua to be strong in Joshua 1:5–9.

> *No man shall be able to stand before you all the days of your life; as I was with Moses, so I will be with you. I will not leave you nor forsake you. Be strong and of good courage, for to this people you shall divide as an inheritance the land which I swore to their fathers to give them. Only be strong and very courageous, that you may observe to do according to all the law which Moses My servant commanded you; do not turn from it to the right hand or to the left, that you may prosper wherever you go. This Book of the Law shall not depart from your mouth, but you shall meditate in it day and night, that you may observe to do according to all that is written in it. For then you will make your way prosperous, and then you will have good success. Have I not commanded you? Be strong and of good courage; do not be afraid, nor be dismayed, for the LORD your God is with you wherever you go.*

Underline or highlight: *As I was with Moses, so I will be with you* and *be strong and of good courage.*

I am encouraged by this remark from author and pastor J. D. Greear: "Christ doesn't call the brave. He makes brave those He calls."[22] God made Moses brave. And this is exactly what we can anticipate God will do for us.

Continue in Joshua 1:5–9. Now underline or highlight at the end: *Be strong and of good courage; do not be afraid, nor be dismayed, for the LORD your God is with you wherever you go.*

Compare the previous passage to Isaiah 41:10 written here: *Fear not, for I am with you; be not dismayed, for I am your God. I will strengthen you, yes, I will help you, I will uphold you with My righteous right hand.*

What does God say He will do in each of these passages?

Just as Edison was fearful of the dark, Moses was afraid to speak. Esther couldn't fathom approaching her king uninvited. The midwives were questioned by Pharoah, and Jochebed had to let her baby go. Yet, God made them all courageous. When darkness surrounds us and we don't know what to do, God will give us courage too.

We will then become a light shining in the darkness. John 1:5 tells us, *The light shines in the darkness, and the darkness did not comprehend it.*

What specifically are you choosing to believe from God's Word today?

Day Four's Sparkling Gem: I believe God will give me the strength and courage to do His will.

Prayer: Powerful God, thank You for Your love and tender care. What You are doing in my life doesn't depend on my strength or wisdom, for I could not bear it. But because of Your strength, I can be bold and courageous. Show me what to do, what to think, what to say, and where to go. I love You! In Jesus's name, amen.

Perspective: Make a list of all your excuses and fears for not accomplishing His will for your life. Commit to fasting for at least one meal and pray over this list, asking God to give you the courage to overcome your fears and minister for Him in a powerful way.

Week One, Day 5

Strength to Stand in Righteousness

People must have righteous principles first, and then they will not
fail to perform virtuous actions.
Martin Luther[23]

Thus says the Lord, your Redeemer, the Holy One of Israel: "I am the Lord your God, who teaches you to profit, who leads you by the way you should go. Oh, that you had heeded My commandments! Then your peace would have been like a river, and your righteousness like the waves of the sea.
Isaiah 48:17–18

Pivotal Point: God gives strength to live a life of integrity.

When my friend Jan moved from Florida to western North Carolina, she brought along an interesting observation. Jan noticed evergreens and other types of trees snap in half or become uprooted in high winds and rain or snowstorms. Comparing the mountain trees to the trees in Florida, she said, "During tropical storms and hurricanes, palm trees bend over—which protects them. When the storm is over, they stand back up."

God is never flippant with His words. With this palm tree insight, we can better understand the comparison of the righteous to trees: the palm tree and cedar.

In fact, let's go to this amazing passage and read it for ourselves. Here's what Psalm 92:12–15 says:

> *The righteous shall flourish like a palm tree, he shall grow like a cedar in Lebanon. Those who are planted in the house of the LORD shall flourish in the courts of our God. They shall still bear fruit in old age; they shall be fresh and flourishing, to declare that the LORD is upright; He is my rock, and there is no unrighteousness in Him.*

In what ways do you flourish and stand like a palm tree?

Reflect on a time you bent in prayer and then stood back up, like a tree or a stately column. What or who gave you the strength to stand? What did you feel inside? If you have not had this experience, ask God to help you encounter "palm tree power."

Why is it essential to bend our independence and self-reliance and humbly ask God to intervene, take control, or provide protection?

How would you explain the connection between bending and standing to a child?

What do you need protection from?

We may have a new appreciation for palm trees when we visit Florida. But there's more.

Oh, thank You, God, for creating us to flourish like a cedar tree!

What, if anything, do you know about cedar trees?

A cedar's roots are firm and deep, symbolizing strength and longevity. And because cedar is resistant to insects, moths, and mold, some people keep precious belongings in cedar chests, hoping they'll last forever—or at least a longer period of time.

We can be confident in this: When God says the righteous will flourish, He will show us how.

The Hebrew word for righteous is *tsaddiq* and means "to be just."[24] Synonyms include blameless or innocent.

There are two words for righteous in the Greek. The word *dikaios* is used when talking about obeying God's commands. Synonyms include: "to be right, be upright."[25] The second Greek word is *teleios* and means "perfect," or "completeness of Christian character."[26]

To be righteous means to have rightness, to be upright, perfect, and complete.

Blameless and perfect? *I can't.* But hang on. Blameless doesn't mean perfect or without sin.

For a deeper understanding, let's begin by reading a passage in the book of Psalms.

Psalm 15:1–2 tells us,

> *Lord, who may dwell in your sacred tent? Who may live on your holy mountain? The one whose walk is blameless, who does what is righteous, who speaks the truth from their heart* (NIV).

During the exodus, God told Moses and Israel to build a large tent. This tent would be the tabernacle where man would meet with God. So, David asks the question:

"Who may come into the sacred tent?" Underline the answer. The New American Standard Bible uses the word *uprightly* in place of *righteous.*

Author and Bible teacher Warren Wiersbe explains blameless as "having to do with soundness of character, integrity, and complete loyalty to God."[27] In this context, blameless means we desire to live by God's laws.

Paul also shed some light on blamelessness. He wrote in Philippians 2:14–15:

> *Do all things without complaining and disputing, that you may*
> *become blameless and harmless, children of God without fault in*
> *the midst of a crooked and perverse generation, among whom you*
> *shine as lights in the world.*

Do you think living a righteous blameless life of integrity is possible? Why or why not? What, if anything, about that command feels difficult?

Can you remember a time when you were pressed to compromise your integrity? What did you do? What steps would you take to guard your integrity the next time this happens?

Return to Psalm 15. Verses 3–5 continue to describe the character of those who may dwell with the Lord. Circle the characteristics.

> *He does not slander with his tongue, nor do evil to his neighbor,*
> *nor bring shame on his friend; a despicable person is despised in*
> *his eyes, but he honors those who fear the LORD; he takes an oath*
> *to his own detriment and does not change; he does not lend his*
> *money at interest, nor does he take a bribe against the innocent.*
> *One who does these things will never be shaken* (NASB).

When we regularly walk with God—meeting Him daily for prayer and Bible reading—we cultivate righteous principles. We speak truth in love and do not commence to bring another person down or break their spirit. Our respect and awe of our Father compels us to live obediently to His Word and avoid shameful and wicked acts. Our desire is to help others, not for our gain or reputation, rather, so others see Jesus.

As Paul described in the previous Philippians verse, this is how we shine.

The Holy Spirit empowers us to stand strong with integrity. And when we do so, we reap benefits. Match the verses to the reference. The benefit (blessing) to us is underlined.

He who walks with integrity walks <u>*securely.*</u>	Psalm 11:7
The integrity of the upright will <u>*guide*</u> *them.*	Psalm 18:23–25
For the LORD is righteous, He loves righteousness; <u>*His countenance beholds*</u> *the upright.*	Psalm 36:10
I was also blameless before Him, and I kept myself from my iniquity. Therefore the LORD has <u>*recompensed me*</u> *according to my righteousness, according to the cleanness of my hands in His sight. With the merciful You will show Yourself merciful; With a blameless man You will show Yourself blameless.*	Psalm 119:1
Oh, continue Your <u>*lovingkindness*</u> *to those who know You, and Your* <u>*righteousness*</u> *to the upright in heart.*	Proverbs 10:9
He who walks in his uprightness <u>*fears*</u> *the LORD.*	Proverbs 11:3
<u>*Blessed*</u> *are those whose way is blameless, who walk in the Law of the LORD* (NASB).	Proverbs 14:2
But seek first the kingdom of God and His righteousness, and <u>*all these things shall be added to you.*</u>	Matthew 6:33

How do you feel knowing the Lord will recompense—compensate and repay you—with blessings for the harm you have suffered? What other benefits stand out to you?

Stand. Stand strong and tall—not only like a palm and cedar, but stately, like a lighthouse on a hill shining the light of Jesus.

What specifically are you choosing to believe from God's Word today?

Day Five's Sparkling Gem: I believe God will give me strength to stand in righteousness.

Prayer: Powerful God, thank You for helping me stand like a palm tree and establish deep roots like a cedar. Thank You for Your protection. Thank You for giving me strength to live a righteous, blameless life, a life that pleases You and brings You glory. In Jesus's name, amen.

Perspective: Purchase a magnet of a palm or cedar tree and place it on your refrigerator or file cabinet. Use this magnet as a reminder that God will strengthen you to stand upright and live righteously. Or for my artsy friends, paint these trees on the front of blank cards. Write Psalm 92:12–15 on the inside.

Participant's Guide

Our beauty reflects the skill of

____.

We're made in the image of

______________________________________.

We're beautiful because

______________________________________.

The beautification process was _______________________________________
and ____.

Myrrh symbolizes the cleansing of

__________________________________.

The young virgins were being prepared to meet

______________________________.

Are you prepared to meet King

_______________________________________?

Introduction: Week Two—She's Beautiful

View Introduction:
Week Two Video on YouTube:

Welcome back! A new or confirmed identity is how the foundation gets built. Embrace your identity and accept the strength God has lavished on you.

This week promises to be another exciting week as we dive deeper into God's Word. Our focus will be on beauty—the beauty in and on us. Let's refresh ourselves with the study's key verse from Psalm 144:12:

> *That our daughters may be as pillars, sculptured in palace style.*

A plain, wooden, or stone column can provide the support to uphold a structure. Yet, the sculptor chisels the column to create something extraordinary, so its beauty reflects the pride and skill of its maker. In the same way, our beauty reflects the skill of our Creator. We're made in the image of Christ; we're beautiful because He is beautiful.

God—the maker of all things beautiful—gave us our senses to experience and appreciate beauty.

- Seeing beauty in the faces of the people we love
- Listening to a symphony
- Tasting something delicious
- Touching textures in fabrics
- Smelling fragrant oils, spices, perfumes, and flowers

Beauty, though, is subjective. Women around the world create opinions based on diverse variables to define what is uniquely beautiful.

In April 2015, Dove, a popular skin care and beauty line, conducted a study. They asked women worldwide to walk through one of two doorways. One door was labeled "Beautiful," and the other door was "Average."

A shocking ninety-six percent of the women walked through the Average Doorway; just four percent considered themselves beautiful.

One participant said, "Beautiful, to me, is too far out of reach."

Another woman confessed, "It was comforting to see these signs, and to have to choose, and be self-conscious of how you perceive yourself and if it lines up with how the rest of the world perceives you."

An American participant added, "Am I choosing because of what is constantly bombarded at me and what I'm being told I should accept? Or am I choosing because that's what I really believe?"[28]

Which doorway would you have passed through? Why?

Beauty is not restricted to physical beauty. Yet skin care companies and Hollywood bombarde us with external beauty products, literally skin deep.

At one time or another, most of us have wrestled with what it means to be a beautiful woman. We wonder if we're beautiful . . . enough. One participant in the Dove survey said, "Knowing it's your decision to feel beautiful is powerful. Once you realize that, no one can make you feel otherwise."

Do you agree that owning your beauty is powerful? Why or why not?

Let's return to our gal Esther with whom we began this study. Scripture tells us Esther was physically beautiful. See this in Esther 2:7.

And Mordecai had brought up Hadassah, that is, Esther, his uncle's daughter, for she had neither father nor mother. The young woman was lovely and beautiful. When her father and mother died, Mordecai took her as his own daughter.

Additionally, we learn the proper beauty protocol in this culture. Read verse twelve:

Each young woman's turn came to go in to King Ahasuerus after she had completed twelve months' preparation, according to the regulations for the women, for thus were the days of their preparation apportioned: six months with oil of myrrh, and six months with perfumes and preparations for beautifying women.

Does this sound like one year of spa treatments to you?

But in the Persian culture, a beautification process was mandated for every girl in the harem: six months in oil of myrrh and six months in spices and ointments.

So, what's special about myrrh?

Myrrh oil was first used as a holy anointing oil in Exodus 20:33. Myrrh was also one of the gifts the wisemen brought to the baby Jesus. Myrrh is a fragrant oil or ointment used in the purification process.[29] Today, modern research has discovered many benefits to oil of myrrh including:

- Antibacterial, antifungal, and astringent agent—for wounds or infection
- Relief for upper respiratory problems—cough and cold relief
- Skin health—soothes chapped skin; also effective for anti-aging, skin rejuvenation, stretch marks, and eczema
- Relaxation—for warm baths and massages
- Mouth health—for fresh breath and oral hygiene
- Cold compress—for swelling and inflammation
- Relieves digestive problems
- Anticancer agent—specifically breast and gynecological cancers[30]

Myrrh is for total body beauty—inside to outside. Don't you just want to take a bath in it?

Me, too! After six months of this kind of beauty treatment, we'd all feel like queens!

There's another side, though. Myrrh comes from the Hebrew word *mor* and means bitterness. [31]

From this perspective, myrrh symbolizes the cleansing of bitterness in our lives. Without this cleansing fragrance, our spiritual lives would have a foul odor.

Hebrews 12:15 tells us, *See to it that no one comes short of the grace of God; that no root of bitterness springing up causes trouble, and by it many become defiled* (NASB).

There's more. During the second six months in the Persian court, the young women continued to be lavished with spices and perfumes. We can only imagine how soothing and lovely this treatment was, since the Bible doesn't expound on it.

The point is the young virgins were being prepared to meet their king.

Are we preparing to meet our king one day? King Jesus?

Esther's gorgeous, exquisite, external beauty initially caught the eye of the king. But over time, her inner beauty was exposed. As she barred all and found favor in the eyes of God, she won again—this time, a place in history.

As queen she was clothed in royalty. As God's obedient daughter, she wore a robe of righteousness. Her words acknowledged God. Her heart was faithful to God and her people. Her mind sought God and He provided her with strategy, wisdom, direction, courage, and problem-solving ability—all necessary in God's plan to rescue the Jews.

During our second week, we'll talk about beauty:

Day 1: Beautiful Mind
Day 2: Beautiful Heart
Day 3: Beautiful Attire
Day 4: Beautiful Fragrance
Day 5: Beautiful Words

Bible commentator Arthur Jackson wrote a woman's "inward virtues and endowments of her mind were her greatest ornament and glory."[32]

Yes!

Let's begin with prayer. I want to share with you a special prayer. You may recall from the introduction that I trusted Jesus as my personal Savior when I was nine years old. I didn't have much theology or spiritual maturity. Neither did I have any fancy words to use in prayers. I used simple language.

Later as I matured and learned more about Bible theology and vocabulary, I could use fancy words in my prayers. But do you know what? I have returned to my nine-year-old's prayer, simply asking God to help me.

God, help me know:

- what to think
- what to say
- what to do
- and where to go

Wherever it is, we'll light up the room with a radiance that reflects Jesus.

Week Two, Day 1

Beautiful Mind

"Watch your thoughts, they become words; watch your words, they become
actions; watch your actions, they become habits; watch your habits, they become
character; watch your character, for it becomes your destiny."
Frank Outlaw[33]

*This Book of the Law shall not depart from your mouth, but you shall meditate in
it day and night, that you may observe to do according to all that is written in it.
For then you will make your way prosperous, and then you will have good
success.*

Joshua 1:8

Pivotal Point: A woman is beautiful when she focuses on God.

In the 2001 movie, *A Beautiful Mind,* John Forbes Nash, a mathematical genius
who suffered with schizophrenia, had to decide what was true and what was not.
In this conversation with his doctor, Mr. Nash is challenged with finding a way to
determine what is real and what isn't:

Dr. Rosen: You can't reason your way out of this!

John Forbes Nash: Why not? Why can't I?

Dr. Rosen: Because your mind is where your problem is in the first
place![34]

Can you relate? Perhaps not as a person with mental challenges, but as a person
with crushing problems on your mind. When I dwell on my troubles, the
negativity inflates like a balloon and consumes so much space in my mind, there's
little room for positivity. My mind becomes off-balanced, with doom and gloom
tipping the scale. The same thing happens when I create fictional problems,
worry, or play with what-if scenarios.

This is not God's best for us. God, the maker of our minds, has given us the
capacity for godly thinking, which ultimately shapes our attitude and determines
our steps.

The Bible tells us in Colossians 3:2, *Set your mind on things above, not on things on the earth.*

What do you think this verse means? Does it mean "heavenly things"? If so, what do you think heavenly things are?

Seems abstract. I mean, how can I look to something invisible?

My mind is busy from the time I get up in the morning, if not before.

What do you think about from the time you get up in the morning to the time you go to bed? Include positive and negative thoughts, plans, ideas, conflicts. We'll come back to this list in a bit.

The story in Matthew 14 of Peter walking on the water is one of the most tangible and effective ways to help us understand this abstract concept.

Jesus asked Peter to walk to Him on water. Peter did. And as long as his eyes were focused on Jesus, he walked. But the moment he looked away and saw the vastness of the sea (the situation), he became afraid and began to sink.

You may wonder what it means to focus on Jesus. From Peter we learn three principles:

- See Jesus in the Word
- Believe Him
- Trust Him

This doesn't imply our eyes won't be blurred with tears. When we focus on God, our thoughts are stabilized, and we are better able to see life through His perspective.

Then, conversation with Him might sound like this:

"God, I need Your perspective on ______________________. (You fill in the blank.) You have never lied to me; You have never failed me. My situation looks bleak, and I'm afraid. But I trust You! You will carry me through this situation and show me what to do. My eyes are fixed on You."

This prayer redirects our concentration from the distraction and problems to the greatness of God's power.

Second Corinthians 10:5 tells us, *Bring[ing] every thought into captivity to the obedience of Christ.*

What do you think it means to take every thought captive?

What thoughts do you need to trap or lock up, so you do not become enslaved by them?

Proverbs 23:7 tells us, *For as [she] thinks in [her] heart, so is [she].*

What thoughts does God want you to think about yourself?

When we focus on God and His perspective, our thoughts align with His, and a beautiful mind grows.

Sometimes, though, our minds become distorted with erroneous information.

Paul, the writer of thirteen books of the New Testament, had his mind reconstructed. He was an educated man, and strict Pharisee who followed the Old Testament's laws. Paul and many other Jews thought New Testament Christ-followers were a threat to the true God because they claimed Jesus was the Savior and Son of God. Believing he was being faithful to God, Paul (at that time named Saul) hunted down the Christians and imprisoned them.

Let's read together in Acts 9:1–22.

What was Saul's intention? (vv. 1–2)

What happened to Saul on his journey to Damascus? (vv. 3–4)

God captured Saul's attention and Saul responded. What was his question? What was God's answer? (vv. 5–6)

Describe the condition of Saul's eyes. (vv. 7–9)

What does God ask Ananias to do? (vv. 10–14)

What happened to Paul's eyes? (vv. 17–18)

What is Saul's new mindset? What does he believe? (v. 22)

By the transforming power of God, Paul's physical and spiritual eyes were opened, and his mind was reprogrammed.

Adjusted. Corrected. A different intellect.

The change was mind blowing.

In Romans 12:2, Paul implores the Christ-followers to have their mind blown too: *And do not be conformed to this world, but be transformed by the renewing of your mind, that you may prove what is that good and acceptable and perfect will of God.*

Don't give in to the world's way of thinking. Resist!

How does transformation begin?

What does this shift in thinking allow us to do?

If our desire is to see things clearly, we'll need a new mindset. Refer to the list you made on the first page of this lesson. Which of your negative thoughts would you like to get rid of?

What specific thought pattern is useless or meaningless?

And fear? Fear is a tool the devil uses to skew the thinking process.

For two and a half years, my incredibly strong husband fought cancer. Ours was equivalent to a hurricane-force storm. Every day we faced unknowns and were challenged with fearful thoughts.

During our painful journey, however, God heard our cries and taught us to guard our hearts.

We learned to focus our thoughts on a great God who has everything under control, who knows what is right and best and good. This mindset did not allow for despair. We clung to many Bible passages. One verse in particular is Philippians 4:7: *The peace of God, which surpasses all understanding, will guard your hearts and minds through Christ Jesus.*

God's peace smothered out fear with calm.

In what area, if any, are you robbed of peace?

Another verse I treasure is Isaiah 26:3: *You will keep him in perfect peace, whose mind is stayed on You, because he trusts in You.*

Stayed. Kept. Daily … hourly … compelled to trust God.

There's no middle ground. We either trust Him or we don't.

Additionally, transformation occurs when we obey what God tells us to think about.

Read Philippians 4:8. What do we think on?

Which thought pattern(s) on the list is most difficult for you?

Which one(s) comes easier?

We may need brain renovation to purge destructive thoughts:

"It's too late to start over with a new mindset. My past follows me and disqualifies me."

Lies from the devil. The Bible says in Philippians 3:13, *Forgetting those things which are behind and reaching forward to those things which are ahead.*

Forgetting events may not be possible, but forgiveness is. Resist the urge to dwell on past failures, struggles, and disappointments. Deal with the bondage of sin and live in freedom.

Holocaust survivor Corrie ten Boom wrote in her book, *Tramp for the Lord:*

> When we confess our sins, God casts them into the deepest ocean, gone forever . . . I believe God then places a sign out there that says No Fishing Allowed.[35]

With a renewed mind, good decisions emerge.

Read Proverbs 31:16 and notice what transpires in this brief verse:

- She thought about, pondered, considered.
- She made her move, bought, invested.
- She acted wisely and turned a profit.

Her level-headed, clear mind enabled her to strategize, problem solve, negotiate, and make wise business decisions.

Whether we're calculating taxes, problem-solving with a teenager, or negotiating with a friend, we need to think clearly.

When I was teaching at a local college, I collaborated with a team on a lengthy accreditation process for our department. Analyzing reports was sometimes tedious and confusing. Many late nights, I prayed and asked God to help me think clearly and solve the problems.

What problem are you solving or troubleshooting?

With whom are you negotiating?

What obstruction do you need to remove?

Second Timothy 1:7 tells us, *For God has not given us a spirit of fear, but of power and of love and of a sound mind.*

Fill in the blanks.

God doesn't give ____________________________.

God gives power, love, and __________________________________.

Some translations use *self-discipline* (NIV), *self-control* (ESV), or *discipline* (NASB), but both the KJV and the NKJV use the term *sound mind.*

The Greek word for "sound mind" is *phroneo* and refers to intelligence and right thinking.[36]

Barnes' Notes on the Bible provides insight on a sound mind:

> The Greek word denotes one of sober mind; a man of prudence and discretion. The state referred to here is that in which the mind is well balanced, and under right influences; in which it sees things in their just proportions and relations.[37]

In other words, God gives us a well-balanced mind and the ability to draw sound conclusions.

Second Corinthians 5:17 says, *Therefore, if anyone is in Christ, he is a new creation; old things have passed away; behold, all things have become new.*

This is great news … if we believe. Believe our mind is made new and functions in a fresh way.

Just like Paul on the Damascus Road, we'll experience the ultimate mind-blowing transformation, which radiates and shines for the glory of God.

Finally, in another scene of *A Beautiful Mind,* John Forbes Nash says, "Perhaps it is good to have a beautiful mind, but [an] even greater gift is to discover a beautiful heart."

Let's take our beautiful minds and proceed to the next chapter, "Beautiful Heart."

What specifically are you choosing to believe from God's Word today?

Day One's Sparkling Gem: I believe my focus on God will transform my thoughts and change my life.

Prayer: Powerful God, thank You for creating my mind. Remove confusion and replace my thoughts with clarity. Help me to problem-solve today and bring You glory. I love You! In Jesus's name, amen.

Perspective: Take Philippians 4:8 a step further. For one week, keep a tally of positive thoughts and negative ones. A self-evaluation can show you where you need to ask God to transform your thinking.

Week Two, Day 2

Beautiful Heart

Since love grows within you, so beauty grows. For love is the beauty of the soul.
Augustine[38]

Now the purpose of the commandment is love from a pure heart, from a good conscience, and from sincere faith, from which some, having strayed, have turned aside to idle talk, desiring to be teachers of the law, understanding neither what they say nor the things which they affirm.
1 Timothy 1:5–6

Pivotal Point: A woman is beautiful when her heart is devoted to God.

Walking with me into my bedroom, Lanie, my four-year-old granddaughter spotted my jewelry box.

"Nana," she asked. "Can I look at your jewelry?"

I put the jewelry box on the floor so she could have a closer look.

Holding a shiny gold heart with a red stone, she asked, "Where did you get this?"

"From your mommy," I replied.

"Why?" she inquired.

"Because she loves me."

Grasping a diamond heart, she asked, "Where did you get this?"

"From your grandfather."

"Why?"

"Because he loves me."

With a sweet but curious countenance, she asked, "Does everybody love you?"

I laughed. "Yes, I suppose they do."

Thoughtfully, she put the jewelry back in the box. With wide eyes, she peered into my eyes and said, "I will bring you something too."[39]

Lanie loves me, so she wanted to bring me something to prove it.

Gift giving is one of the many ways we show others our love.

I love God. I wish I could hand Him a gift!

God has designed women with the capacity to love Him fully. The Bible tells us in Matthew 22:37, *You shall love the LORD your God with all your heart, with all your soul, and with all your mind.*

Often, though, I wonder if the words of my heart are in sync with my actions.

The story of Mary and Martha recorded in Luke 10:38–42 grips my heart. Likely, you're familiar with this account. Perhaps you've been branded as one of these two women, based on your style and personality.

But let's walk through this short passage together and observe the unique gifts of both women. Read this passage and answer the following questions.

Who welcomed Jesus into their home? (v. 38) What do you think her countenance might have been? What can you envision were her words?

Who was Martha's sister, and where was she positioned? (v. 39) Which of her senses were engaged?

Why do you think Martha continued to serve? What was on her mind? What does she ask Jesus to do? (v. 40)

How many times did He say her name? (v. 41) What did Jesus say was the good part? (v. 42)

Oh Martha, I do like you!

Martha's friendly, service-driven, problem-solving style traits bubble up and spill over from her caring, compassionate heart.

And Mary. I long to be like you.

Gentle, tender. Observant. Mary wasn't about to miss her time with the Savior.

With which of these two women do you most identify?

If Jesus wasn't dismissing Martha's gift of hospitality, what do you think He meant?

What is the lesson about priorities?

A moment ago, you were asked which woman you were most like. Did this question confuse you because you felt you were a bit like both?

Me, too!

Oh, girl, this is very good! When we put activity aside to spend time with Jesus in prayer and Bible study, then get busy using our gifts to accomplish God's plan and purpose, we're representing both of these women's qualities.

Starting our day with a Mary heart enables us to be effective and productive with our Martha work.

Be Mary first, then be Martha.

The Bible tells us in Proverbs 3:6, *In all your ways acknowledge Him, and He shall direct your paths.*

A Mary heart and a Martha heart. There's no debate. We can have both.

Underline what is our part. Put a box around God's part.

How would you paraphrase Proverbs 3:6 in everyday language?

There's more sweetness coming.

Picture this moment: *"Martha, Martha."*

When Jesus spoke Martha's name twice, He was displaying intimacy and friendship. He used a gentle reproof and a special tenderness in the repetition of her name.[40]

Aww.

Our turn.

Print your name in both blanks. Then envision Jesus speaking to you.

"_______________________, _______________________, you are distracted and worried with many things."

How did writing your name in the blank make you feel?

These sweet sisters had different styles, but Jesus had both their hearts.

Another group of people *appeared* to love God. You might be familiar with this group as well: the scribes and Pharisees.

In case you're unfamiliar with the scribes' and Pharisees' jobs, here's a description:

Scribes—Lawyers and teachers of the law. They weren't a religious sect but a class of professional scholars. Their expertise in explaining the law and applying it to everyday circumstances allowed them to hand down legal decisions.

Pharisees—These were members of a Jewish religious sect, the most prominent group among the religious leaders. They emphasized the importance of keeping God's rules.[41]

The Gospels frequently list the two together.

To onlookers, the scribes and Pharisees appeared to have hearts truly devoted to God. But Jesus saw through their external appearance and condemned their dirty hearts. See for yourself in Matthew 23:1–34.

Match the religious leaders' sins to the references in Matthew 23. (Two have the same verse.)

vv. 1–3, v. 4, vv. 5–7. vv. 13–14, v. 15, vv. 16–22, vv. 23–24, vv. 25–28, vv. 29–34

________ They tell others what to do, but they don't live by the same rules.

________ They inflict heavy burdens on the people but refuse to help them.

________ They strap leather boxes of Scripture to their arms and forehead to show off.

________ They attend the feasts, but selfishly insist on the best seat.

________ They exempt themselves from God's law.

________ They offer false salvation, so the person lived far worse than before.

________ They look for ways to break oaths.

________ They obsess over petty rules but neglect mercy, justice, and faith.

________ They cleanse the outside to look good, but their interior is dirty.

________ They murdered the prophets but felt worthy to sit in Moses's seat of authority.

The word *woe* means "God's judgment, grief, and denunciation."[42] Between verses 13–36, how many times did Jesus say, "woe"?

Jesus saw through the scribes' and Pharisees' arrogant, self-serving acts and exposed them. He recognized their filthy hearts—their true motives and thoughts. First Samuel 16:7 tells us, *But the LORD said to Samuel, "Do not look at his appearance or at his physical stature, because I have refused him. For the LORD does not see as man sees; for man looks at the outward appearance, but the LORD looks at the heart."*

The scribes and Pharisees didn't love God as much as they loved themselves. We can fool people, but we can't fool God.

None of us want to hear the words, "woe to you" the way the Pharisees did. God wants to help us with any heart condition. When God lovingly shows us hidden sin, we can seek forgiveness.

Psalm 51:16–17 says:

> *For You do not desire sacrifice, or else I would give it; You do not delight in burnt offering. The sacrifices of God are a broken spirit, a broken and a contrite heart—these, O God, You will not despise.*

The dictionary defines *contrite* as someone who shows sincere remorse.[43]

Is there anything in your heart you need to release to God?

What do you want to be in your heart?

The New Living Translation paraphrases Proverbs 3:3–4 this way:

> *Never let loyalty and kindness leave you! Tie them around your neck as a reminder. Write them deep within your heart. Then you will find favor with both God and people, and you will earn a good reputation.*

And Acts 13:22 tells us, *I have found David the son of Jesse, a man after My own heart, who will do all My will.*

Mary and Martha loved God with their whole heart and did His will. The scribes and Pharisees faked their loyalty. What do you think made David a man after God's heart?

David didn't have God's heart because of his position as king of Israel but because of his habits. We too can be described as a "woman after God's heart" when we practice David's habits:

- When David sinned, he confessed.
- He inquired of God when he needed help.
- When he was sad, he cried and was authentic before God.
- David rejoiced in God despite his circumstances.
- When he didn't understand, he still praised God.
- When David was afraid, he continued to thank God.
- He delighted in God's Word.
- David sought God and obeyed.
- He trusted God.

How would you rate the condition of your heart? Is it devoted like Mary's or busy like Martha's? Is it disillusioned like the scribes' and Pharisees' or obedient like David's?

If you're unsure, or need a reset, you're in a good place. We all are. We can make Psalm 51:10 our prayer: *Create in me a clean heart, O God, and renew a steadfast spirit within me.*

We have the promise of forgiveness found in Psalm 32:5: *I acknowledged my sin to You, and I did not hide my guilt; I said, "I will confess my wrongdoings to the LORD"; and You forgave the guilt of my sin* (NASB).

How lovely and inviting.

Like Lanie, who desired to give a gift conveying her love, we can give God a gift:

- A heart devoted to Him
- A heart expressing remorse for sin and a sincere desire for change
- A heart to obey Him

Psalm 24:3–4 asks, *Who may ascend into the hill of the Lord? And who may stand in His holy place? He who has clean hands and a pure heart.*

Oh, girl, because of God's great love for us, our beautiful hearts can beam for Him.

What specifically are you choosing to believe from God's Word today?

Day Two's Sparkling Gem: I believe my heart is beautiful and my reputation is radiant when my heart is devoted, repentant, and obedient to God.

Prayer: Loving Father, I give to You my heart—my whole heart. The good parts, the hard parts, the confusion, and the wrong motives. I confess my sin and look forward to a new beginning today! Help me be devoted. Give me strength to be obedient. I love You! In Jesus's name I pray, amen.

Perspective: If you wear jewelry, you can wear a heart-shaped pendant around your neck or attach it to your shirt or jacket as a reminder. Or purchase a heart-shaped ring. If jewelry isn't your thing, acquire a heart magnet. Any of these items will prompt you to do a daily heart check.

Week Two, Day 3

Beautiful Attire

The flower of youth never appears more beautiful than when it bends toward the
sun of righteousness.
Matthew Henry[44]

Bless the LORD, *O my soul! O* LORD *my God, You are very great: You are clothed
with honor and majesty, who cover Yourself with light as with a garment, who
stretch out the heavens like a curtain.*
Psalm 104:1–2

Pivotal Point: A woman is beautiful when she is clothed in righteousness.

The world of fashion is a multi-billion-dollar industry. Our clothes may define
who we are—and our preferred colors, textures, and styles. What we put on also
identifies who we are for the moment: an athlete, for example, or a corporate
executive. Even pajamas clarify our intentions. Our changing moods can also
influence what we wear.

I love hues and textures and find joy in putting on an attractive outfit, especially
one that compliments the color of my eyes.

Have you ever thought about what God wears? How do you imagine God?

The Bible gives us a picture-perfect description of God. One example is Psalm
93:1–2, which says,

> *The* LORD *reigns, He is clothed with majesty; the* LORD *is clothed,
> He has girded Himself with strength. Surely the world is
> established, so that it cannot be moved. Your throne is established
> from of old; You are from everlasting.*

Majesty. A familiar word most of us heard throughout childhood in fairy tales.

Aww. Curtesy to the queen and address her as "Your Majesty."

Webster's Dictionary defines majesty as "sovereign power, authority, or dignity."[45] In the context of God, the Hebrew word *hod* is used for majesty and means authority, honor, and splendor.[46]

Don't you think "splendor" has a pleasant sound? Based on the above passage in Psalm 104:1–2 and the Hebrew meaning of majesty, how is God clothed?

God's wardrobe reveals His character, and His creation unwraps His glory.

> *Consider how the wild flowers grow. They do not labor or spin. Yet I tell you, not even Solomon in all his splendor was dressed like one of these* (Luke 12:27 NIV).

God, His wardrobe, and His glory are magnificent and everlasting.

Conversely, our external covering is temporary. We might shine externally for a day. But eventually, the threads on our clothing will unravel and the fabric will rip and fade. Wrinkles and age spots will dull our once bright skin.

Only our spiritual wardrobe—our internal radiance—shines from within and is attractive forever.

Amazing. We are beautifully designed to reflect His glory forever!

Let's look together at one nameless woman who is identified in Scripture as truly beautiful and virtuous. Read Proverbs 31:10–31. Match the description to the verse.

For her worth is far above rubies (v. 10)

Thoughtful __________

The heart of her husband safely trusts her (v. 11)

Provider __________

She does him good and not evil (v. 12)

Worker __________

Willingly works with her hands
(v.13)

Good ___________

She also rises while it is yet night,
And provides food for her
household (v. 15)

Trustworthy ___________

She considers a field and buys it
(v. 16)

Worthy ___________

From her profits she plants a
vineyard (v.16)

Respectful ___________

She girds herself with strength
(v. 17)

Wise decision-maker ___________

Her clothing is fine linen and
purple (v. 22)

Honorable___________

Strength and honor are her
clothing (v.25)

Kind___________

She opens her mouth with
wisdom And on her tongue is the
law of kindness (v. 26)

Attractive___________

She watches over the ways of her
household, And does not eat the
bread of idleness (v. 27)

Time-manager___________

Charm is deceitful and beauty is
passing, but a woman who fears
the Lord, she shall be praised
(v.30)

Strong ___________

Huh.

This virtuous woman might appear intimidating. Yet we can also cultivate these
honorable character traits.

If we feel like a hopeless mess, all torn and ragged, stripped of dignity, we need a reset.

Let's go shopping for it. We don't have to travel far—only to a quiet place in our house or yard where we can invest additional time in God's Word.

Isaiah 61:10 tells us,

> *I will greatly rejoice in the LORD, my soul shall be joyful in my God; for He has clothed me with the garments of salvation, He has covered me with the robe of righteousness, as a bridegroom decks himself with ornaments, and as a bride adorns herself with her jewels.*

Circle, star, or put hearts around this phrase: *He has covered me with the robe of righteousness.*

Righteousness. Made right with God and able to do rightly.

Imagine. You're curled up like a baby feeling less-than and without purpose. Suddenly, like a warm blanket, God takes His cloak of righteousness and drapes it around you.

Aww. Warm acceptance.

Do you identify as a woman clothed in righteousness? Why or why not?

In what ways has God exchanged your rags for a righteous robe?

It sounds profound. Yet it's so simple and sincere.

The LORD says, "Turn to Me with all your heart, with fasting, with weeping, and with mourning." So rend your heart, and not your garments; return to the LORD your God, for He is gracious and merciful, slow to anger, and of great kindness; and He relents from doing harm (Joel 2:12–13).

Rend. Huh.

Merriam-Webster's Dictionary defines *rend* as tearing or splitting.[47] The tearing of one's clothes is an ancient tradition among the Jews and is associated with humility, mourning, grief, and loss. In ancient times, tearing one's clothes was a public and powerful expression of grief.

> "The practice is continued today in the Jewish practice of *keriah*. Today's ritual is less spontaneous and more regulated: the garment is cut by a rabbi at a funeral service, as the bereaved recite words relating to God's sovereignty. One tradition says that the mourner must tear the clothing over the heart—a sign of a broken heart."[48]

The prophet Joel, however, said, "Rend your heart and not your garments." It's more important to show genuine repentance of the heart rather than to perform an external ritual.

We can speak our filthy rags away when we repent of our sin and make Jesus our Lord: *"Take away the filthy garments from him." And to him He said, "See, I have removed your iniquity from you, and I will clothe you with rich robes"* (Zechariah 3:4).

Let's move over to the New Testament and read in Philippians 3:13–14. With this passage in clear view, what do you need to leave behind?

God is concerned with the influence of our past, but He is focused on the future—specifically, *your* future. Do you believe God forgives your filthy, ragged past and is preparing you to be fit for a palace? Why or why not?

This is so good!

See for yourself. Read Revelation 19:8. What fine linen of righteous acts (doing what is right) are you wearing?

Also read Isaiah 11:5. What makes you stand out in the crowd?

For clarity, let's study together what works, or acts, of righteousness we can put on each day.

Go with me to Colossians 3:8–9, 12–14. On the left space of the chart, list at least five things to put on. Circle what we should take off. Then go to Ephesians 4:25–5:2 and do the same thing.

Colossians 3:8–9, 12–14	Ephesians 4:25–5:2
List at least five things to put on:	List at least five things to put on:
1.	1.
2.	2.
3.	3.
4.	4.
5.	5.

<table>
<tr><td>Take off:

anger   wrath   malice   hate

blasphemy   lies   love

meanness   humility   joy

filthy language

desire to inflict pain

lack of reverence for God</td>
<td>Take off:

Truth   lying   anger   stealing

wrath   work   love   malice

peace   clamor   bitterness

evil speaking   corrupt talk</td></tr>
</table>

Let's take an honest look at what's hanging in our spiritual closet.

Do you need to discard any garments? If so, which ones?

Is an essential item missing?

Do you think attitude is something we wear? Why or why not?

Let's wrap up with what Peter says in 1 Peter 3:3–4:

> *Do not let your adornment be merely outward—arranging the hair, wearing gold, or putting on fine apparel—rather let it be the hidden person of the heart, with the incorruptible beauty of a gentle and quiet spirit, which is very precious in the sight of God.*

The Greek word for adorn is *kosmeo* which means to "make ready, prepare, or embellish with honor."[49]

Peter stresses that we don't *just* get dressed externally but also strive to make our internal adornment a priority.

Something to think about: Is your plain or drab look your preference, or is it a false modesty? Is your fancier or brighter look your preference or a false superiority? Either style is okay if we don't use our choice as a reason to judge someone else's. Neither should we allow our preference to divert attention from our inner beauty.

What else is a priority? Turn to 1 Peter 5:5 and fill in the blank.

Dress/clothe yourself in ____.

Humility means we're not preoccupied with ourselves; rather, we give God credit—the glory—for what He does through us.

Reflect on one thing you've done well or been given praise for. How do you stay humble and give God credit for this praise?

Psalm 149:4 tells us, *For the LORD takes pleasure in His people; He will beautify the humble with salvation.*

When we accept God's gift of salvation, He removes our spiritual rags and drapes us in garments of righteousness. And this new wardrobe enables us to shine like stars in the sky.

Our wardrobe smells wonderful too. On Day Four, we'll get a whiff of true beauty.

What specifically are you choosing to believe from God's Word today?

Day Three's Sparkling Gem: I believe my robe of righteousness enables me to shine with an unfading beauty.

Prayer: Father, thank You for my new wardrobe. Give me strength each day to put on righteous acts and attitudes. Give me wisdom, discretion, and discernment. Help me recall what I need to take off and put on. When I see rags, help me remember You have dressed me in Your robe of righteousness on me. Help me disregard the temporal and focus rather on the eternal. In Jesus's name, amen.

Perspective: Take an old t-shirt or shirt you no longer wear and, starting at the bottom, use scissors to cut strips up to the chest, leaving the shoulders intact. Then hang this rag on a hanger, as a reminder you no longer wear rags.

Week Two, Day 4

Beautiful Fragrance

*Therefore be imitators of God as dear children. And walk in love, as Christ also
has loved us and given Himself for us, an offering and a sacrifice to God for a
sweet-smelling aroma.*
Ephesians 5:1–2

Pivotal Point: A woman is beautiful when she disperses the fragrance of life.

"I knew it was you," declared the third grader as he walked into the classroom
where I was the substitute teacher. "I could smell you!"

I laughed. When my children were young, they said the same thing.

Not everyone enjoys the scent of perfume. However, according to one survey,
these are among the world's best aromas:

- the smell of baked bread
- warm cookies straight from the oven
- freshly brewed coffee
- a summer rain shower
- vanilla
- cut grass[51]

Sometimes certain fragrances create pictures in our minds; they have the power to
transport us to a different time. When I was burning a honeysuckle candle, my
husband told me the scent carried him back to summers when he was a child,
playing in the woods and running through pastures.

What fragrance makes you feel good, pulls at your heartstrings, or reminds you of
something beautiful?

Perhaps you're thinking, I don't wear any fragrances and am intolerant of fabricated or synthetic smells, so this chapter doesn't apply to me.

Oh, but it does.

Christ-followers release a spiritual scent. Our spiritual aroma will either repel or attract others to the One we follow.

Let's talk about godly fragrances. Second Corinthians 2:14–16 tells us:

> *Now thanks be to God who always leads us in triumph in Christ, and through us diffuses the fragrance of His knowledge in every place. For we are to God the fragrance of Christ among those who are being saved and among those who are perishing. To the one we are the aroma of death leading to death, and to the other the aroma of life leading to life. And who is sufficient for these things?*

The gospel message is like incense diffused everywhere. Those who live for Christ share the gospel and emit His love. This lovely scent, the fragrance of new life in Christ, rises to the Father. Those who reject Christ reject the fragrance and the result is death. The more we mature in the faith, the more we become the fragrance of new life.

Do you think others smell the fragrance of Christ in our organization or church? Why or why not?

Do others smell the gospel in you? Maybe you can't answer because you're unsure you have new life. If this is your situation, go to Appendix A—How to Make a Decision For Jesus—and take your first step towards beauty: accept the gospel and salvation and confirm your belief in Jesus.

Fragrances hold significant meaning in the Bible. In the Old Testament, for example, God told priests to burn aromatic incense made of an exotic spice blend. The ancient Israelites also offered sacrifices—a sweet aroma to the Lord. Leviticus chapter two describes distinct types of sacrifices:

- Meat offering/burnt offering—animal sacrifices offered for the atonement (remission) of sin.

- Wheat offering—fine grain offered for worship.
- Meal offering—vegetable sacrifice consisting of flour and salt usually mingled with oil and frankincense.[52]

The fragrance of the sacrifices was pleasing to God because it signified obedience, repentance, worship, love, and devotion.

In the New Testament, Jesus's shed blood became the one-time sacrifice for us all. The ultimate beautiful fragrance was emitted when:

> *He [Jesus Christ] was pierced for our transgressions, [and] he was crushed for our iniquities; the punishment that brought us peace was on him, and by his wounds we are healed.* (Isaiah 53:5 NIV)

The most costly fragrance issued from Jesus's crushing on the cross. The scent produced was love.

Let's journey through an extraordinary story in Matthew 26:6–13 and discover a woman who produced the fragrance of devotion. Answer the following questions about Mary of Bethany:

What did *this woman* have? What did she do with it? (v. 7)

What did the disciples say about her actions and what did they express would have been better? (vv. 8–9)

How did Jesus respond? (vv. 10–11)

This woman, later identified as Mary, the sister of Martha and Lazarus (John 11:1– 2) was a devoted follower of Jesus. She pondered His teachings and the events she had witnessed—namely, her brother Lazarus's resurrection. Now, before Passover, Mary sought His heart.

Matthew 26:12 says Mary anointed Jesus's head with expensive, fragrant perfume as a prophetic significance—preparing His body for death.

Hmm. Was Mary so close to Jesus she predicted His death was near?

We may never know. But we can agree that Mary's act was a beautiful example of adoration.

Read about another fragrant anointing in Luke 7:36–50. Then answer the following questions:

Where were they gathered? (v. 36)

What did the woman bring? (v. 37)

What three things did she do to cleanse Jesus's feet? (v. 38)

How does the Pharisee describe this woman? (v. 39)

What was Jesus's reprimand to Simon? (vv. 44–46)

What does Jesus tell this woman with a sinful reputation? (vv. 48–50)

How are these stories similar?

Humility. Worship. Love and devotion. A sweet-smelling aroma to God.

Sometimes, though, what we offer to God, stinks. Consider Isaiah 65:1–2, 5:

> *I was sought by those who did not ask for Me; I was found by those who did not seek Me. I said, 'Here I am, here I am,' to a nation that was not called by My name. I have stretched out My hands all day long to a rebellious people, who walk in a way that is not good, according to their own thoughts. These are smoke in My nostrils, a fire that burns all the day.*

The New Living Translation uses *stench* instead of *smoke*. Why did God have a foul smell in His nose?

We may not want to face this reality, but have you ever thought about what God smells when He gets a whiff of you? What is your scent? (for example: humility, worship, love, devotion, obedience, repentance.)

What do you want your fragrance to be?

Our fragrance is significant, first to God, and second to others.

Do we smell different? What does new life smell like? Second Corinthians 5:17 says, *Therefore, if anyone is in Christ, he is a new creation; old things have passed away; behold, all things have become new.*

When others get a sniff of us, may they smell the aroma of new life, not the stench of death or darkness. Is the scent we exude nauseating or uplifting? If onlookers smell in us hopelessness, anger, immorality, godlessness, impurity, hate, or revenge, they won't desire the God we say we have. Nor will they yearn for a God who is untrustworthy or one who abandons His children.

Ephesians 4:1 tells us to, *Walk worthy of the calling with which you were called,* and First Peter 3:15 says, *Always be ready to give a defense to everyone who asks you a reason for the hope that is in you.*

Walk. A continuous movement. A habitual lifestyle.

A devotion to God points others to Him.

What needs to die in your life so you can emit a life-giving fragrance to those around you?

Let's make the choice. We can be the perfume representing life with Christ.

What specifically are you choosing to believe from God's Word today?

Day Four's Sparkling Gem: I believe when my heart is devoted to Jesus Christ, I emit a beautiful fragrance.

Prayer: Oh Father, God, I desire to be smothered in the fragrance of Jesus Christ. Teach me. Guide me. Show me. Help me. I want to be a fragrant candle burning bright in a murky world, showing others the Way, the Truth, and the Life. In Jesus's name, amen.

Perspective: If you can tolerate synthetic smells, pick a favorite candle or an oil diffuser to remind you that we all emit a fragrance. You might even try out myrrh oil. The fragrance—symbolic of love, devotion, worship, humility, repentance, and obedience—blossoms when we spend time in God's Word and in prayer.

Week Two, Day 5

Beautiful Words

Words which do not give the light of Christ increase the darkness.
Mother Teresa[53]

Let the words of my mouth and the meditation of my heart be acceptable in Your sight, O LORD, my strength and my Redeemer.
Psalm 19:14

Pivotal Point: A woman is beautiful when her words praise God and bring healing and to others.

Words are powerful. Beautiful words in particular transform people and their lives. They inspire, challenge, and move us.

Did you know there are lists comprising the most beautiful words in the world? Of course, a beautiful word is subjective, but one list included these words: invigorating, heartfelt, and mellifluous.

Mellifluous?

This Latin word is defined a: "a sound pleasing and sweet to hear."[54] We all have our preferences for what words we consider to be lovely, but what verbiage, utterances, expressions, or conversations do you think God considers beautiful?

Using Our Words to Edify God

You can imagine the beautiful sound waves that shook heaven when Mary, the mother of Jesus, broke out in song and praise to God her Father. I realize we're reading words printed on paper, but read this passage aloud and listen to an excerpt of Mary's words found in Luke 1:46–55:

> *"My soul magnifies the Lord, and my spirit has rejoiced in God my Savior ...For He who is mighty has done great things for me, and*

81

*holy is His name. And His mercy is on those who fear Him ... He
has shown strength with His arm ... He has filled the hungry with
good things ...He has helped His servant Israel, in remembrance
of His mercy ... "*

From this passage, we can infer that Mary loves God. What does Mary think
about God? What specific words show her worshipful attitude?

And then there's Hannah, the mother of Samuel.

How privileged we are to hear Hannah's God-honoring prayer in 1 Samuel 2:1–
10:

*And Hannah prayed and said: "My heart rejoices in the LORD; my
horn [strength] is exalted in the LORD... No one is holy like the
LORD, for there is none besides You, nor is there any rock like our
God ... for the LORD is the God of knowledge; and by Him actions
are weighed ... and those who stumbled are girded with strength
... and the hungry have ceased to hunger. Even the barren has
borne seven ... He raises the poor from the dust ... For the pillars
of the earth are the LORD's, and He has set the world upon them.
He will guard the feet of His saints ...The LORD will judge the ends
of the earth. He will give strength to His king and exalt the horn
[strength] of His anointed. "*

Full of praise, Hannah doesn't hold back. Gratitude and adoration pour out from
her soul.

How does Hannah describe God?

Words of praise, worship, and gratitude—whether signed with our hands, written,
spoken, or texted, are beautiful to the Lord.

How about King David? You probably know some of David's story, like how in his earlier years he was often on the run from jealous King Saul. And David suffered the consequences of his sin, too.

Did he praise God? Always. Just look at what he penned in Psalm 145! Read this passage at your convenience but to get you excited, verses 1–3 are written here:

> *I will extol You, my God, O King; and I will bless Your name*
> *forever and ever. Every day I will bless You, and I will praise Your*
> *name forever and ever. Great is the LORD, and greatly to be*
> *praised; and His greatness is unsearchable.*

Are you in the habit of praise? If yes, for what do you praise God? If no, would you like to cultivate the habit of praise?

When I became an adult, my mom told me she slept with her Bible on her chest. As a divorcee in the 1970s, Mom often felt alone, different, and fearful. Gripping her Bible brought her hope and comfort.

My mom had many favorite passages, but she read aloud 1 Chronicles 29:11–13:

> *Yours, O LORD, is the greatness, the power and the glory, the*
> *victory and the majesty; for all that is in heaven and in earth is*
> *Yours; Yours is the kingdom, O LORD, and You are exalted as head*
> *over all. Both riches and honor come from You, and You reign*
> *over all. In Your hand is power and might; in Your hand it is to*
> *make great and to give strength to all. Now therefore, our God, we*
> *thank You and praise Your glorious name.*

My mom was beautiful because of her words of praise to God.

Today when you and I don't know what to pray or say to God, we can read one of the above passages. Beginning our day with praise is beautiful.

Using Our Words to Edify Others

The Bible also gives ample direction on how to use words to encourage and edify others.

Ephesians 4:29 says: *Do not let any unwholesome talk come out of your mouths, but only what is helpful for building others up according to their needs, that it may benefit those who listen* (NIV).

Depending on the Bible translation you used, you may have read *edification* which means building up. Is building up or encouraging others a challenge for you? Why or why not? What are ways you can encourage others with either your spoken or written words?

The word translated as *unwholesome* in this verse literally means "rotten." The English Standard Version uses the word *corrupt*, and the Revised Standard Version uses *evil*. The New Living Translation renders the verse this way:

> *Don't use foul or abusive language. Let everything you say be good and helpful, so that your words will be an encouragement to those who hear them.*

Circle the words *foul* and *abusive*. Today, abusive language is also considered a form of emotional abuse. Look here at synonyms for *foul* and the definition of *abusive*:

Foul: Offensive, obscene, abusive, detestable, vulgar, or insulting language.

Abusive: "Using harsh, insulting language; emotional cruelty"[55]

For some people, using foul or abusive language is a habit. Maybe they grew up with this type of language in the home or live in a culture where this kind of language is socially acceptable.

Maybe you struggle in these areas or know someone who does.

How can a foul mouth detract from a Christian's witness?

The above passage says our words should build others up according to their need and encourage them. Do you think gossip is encouragement, or does it qualify as a form of abuse? Why or why not?

Let's go to the Old Testament and read Proverbs 15:1–4. Compare how Scripture identifies words as good or evil.

Words are good when:

    1.

    2.

    3.

Words are evil when:

    1.

    2.

    3.

Squished in the middle of this passage are these words *The eyes of the LORD are in every place, keeping watch on the evil and the good.* A timely reminder. He sees. He hears.

Think about these questions so you'll be better prepared the next time a situation arises:

How can I phrase words to avoid an angry blowup? (Keep in mind, another person's response to your words is between God and them and the outcome isn't always up to you.)

What information might I need to have before I speak?

In what way can I bring life-giving words of encouragement, guidance, or truth?

As Christ-followers and women polished and fit for a palace, we can bring cheer to another person's life. There's immense potential to bring healing and life. Match these references to the amazing Scriptures.

__ Job 4:4

A. *She opens her mouth in wisdom, and the teaching of kindness is on her tongue.*

__ Proverbs 12:25

B. *Anxiety in a man's heart weighs it down, but a good word makes it glad.*

__ Proverbs 15:4

C. *Pleasant words are as a honeycomb, sweet to the soul, and health to the bones.*

__ Proverbs 15:23

D. *Your words have helped the tottering to stand, and you have strengthened feeble knees.*

__ Proverbs 16:24

E. *A soothing tongue is a tree of life.*

__ Proverbs 31:26

F. *A man has joy in an apt answer, and how delightful is a timely word!*

__ Colossians 4:6

G. *Let your speech always be gracious, seasoned with salt, so that you may know how you ought to answer each person.*

Spread good words and light up someone's life. (Psalm 119:130, paraphrased).

What specifically are you choosing to believe from God's Word today?

Day Five's Sparkling Gem: I believe my words praise God and bring life and light to others.

Prayer: Wonderful, mighty God! You are my Savior, my constant hope. You go before me and defend me. You uphold me with Your righteous right hand. You are creator of all things, and You know me perfectly! You are powerful and just. You are compassionate, kind, and loving! You are all I need. I love You! In Jesus's name, amen.

Perspective: Studies say it takes twenty-one days to stop or start a habit. Let's start a good one today. For twenty-one days, make a list of what you are thankful for and then read your list to God. Praise Him for what He's done in your life and for His faithfulness to you. After twenty-one days, start the cycle again, then keep going until praise becomes a habit.

<u>**Introduction: Week Three- She's Wise**</u>

Participant's Guide

Understanding God's design for women cultivates a _______________ _______________ within our soul.

To me, wisdom is

____.

Solomon personifies

____.

The implication is that a woman's outreach is

_______________________________________.

With wisdom, women _______________________, _______________________,
And structure _______________, _______________________, and
_______________.

The seven pillars of wisdom are:

Fear _______________________________

K_______________________________

U_______________________________

I_______________________________

D_______________________________

Counsel and _______________________

P_______________________________

When Esther fasted and prayed, she demonstrated

____.

Although Esther was in a powerful position, she demonstrated

______________________________.

When Esther devised a plan, she demonstrated

____.

She had a lot at stake, yet she demonstrated

____.

When Esther approached the king at the right time, she demonstrated

____________________.

When Esther obeyed God she demonstrated

____.

View Introduction:
Week Three Video on YouTube:

Deep breath.

Close your eyes and inhale hope.

Exhale uniqueness.

It's overwhelming, isn't it? Believing we're exceptional. Distinct. Worthy.

Our part of Psalm 144:12—*That our daughters may be as pillars, sculptured in palace style*—is only eleven words.

Eleven words.

A short phrase with significant impact. In fact, life altering.

The way God uses *daughters* and *pillars* in the same sentence makes us smile. We're strong, created on purpose and with purpose. Understanding God's design for women cultivates God-confidence within our soul.

Believe it.

In less than two weeks, we've seen women who live by biblical principles manifest God-infused strength and beauty.

Today we'll continue to examine the meaning of *pillar*. Matthew Henry's Commentary, the most widely used Bible commentary, sheds light on this word. He says:

> By daughters, families are united and connected, to their mutual strength, as the parts of a building are by the corner stones ... we see our daughters well-established and stayed with wisdom and discretion, as corner stones are fastened in the building ... we see them purified and consecrated to God as living temples.[56]

Henry's compelling words deepen our understanding. When women are dependent on the multi-faceted wisdom from God, they become a cornerstone, holding it together. And a pillar who stands, though everything around her is crumbling.

What visual or symbol comes to your mind when you hear the word *wisdom*?

Is it an owl or gray hair? Maybe you've heard wisdom described in other ways, too. But I like to visualize wisdom as an elaborate staircase ascending to heaven. To me, wisdom is running to God's throne.

Did you realize God intends for us to have wisdom? He designed us with the capacity to be wise. He tells us this truth in James 1:5: *If any of you lacks wisdom, let him ask of God, who gives to all liberally and without reproach, and it will be given to him.*

Is James referring to the scholars only? Or a select few? No. The verse says *any of you* and *all.*

Not all, however, choose to receive it.

I confess. Even though I've known wisdom is available, I often don't search for it. When I was a younger woman and growing in my faith, praying for wisdom was more like a routine or habit. I asked God to cover me with general wisdom in all areas of my life. Asking in this way isn't necessarily wrong, but a decade ago something happened, and my quest for wisdom went from general to specific.

I urgently needed to make a vital decision regarding my mom's health care and rehabilitation options. With only days until decision time, I was overwhelmed with the choices—and the fear of making the wrong decision. On a Sunday night, I poured out my heart to God.

"I need wisdom to know what to do," I managed to say through my sobbing.

"I boldly come before the throne of grace asking for the wisdom You said You'd give! I'm going to pray intentionally and specially morning, noon, and night until You show me what to do. But also, provide my mom with the same wisdom so we're in complete agreement. And we must have it now."

My earnest prayer continued for two days. On the second day of visiting my mom in the hospital, we prayed together.

Then Mom smiled and said she had something to tell me.

"Last night I had a dream. I was in a room with a large picture window. Fall flowers were growing in the garden, and I could see birds eating at the feeders. I told the nurse my daughter would come decorate the sterile-looking room and make it more attractive."

My mom looked into my eyes.

"God showed me in a dream what we need to do and where I should go," she said.

God gave both my mother and me the wisdom to make the right choice. We hugged and cried tears of joy. The wisdom God provided filled us with peace.

After that specific answer to my request, I wondered why I hadn't prayed boldly for wisdom in other areas of my life.

The book of Proverbs is a treasure chest of wisdom. Solomon, the son of David, king of Israel, wrote most of the content. Beginning in chapter one and continuing through chapter nine, Solomon personifies wisdom as a woman.

Let's read Proverbs 1:20–23:

> *Wisdom calls aloud outside; she raises her voice in the open squares. She cries out in the chief concourses, at the openings of the gates in the city she speaks her words: "How long, you simple ones, will you love simplicity? For scorners delight in their scorning, and fools hate knowledge. Turn at my rebuke; Surely I will pour out my spirit on you; I will make my words known to you.*

Now skip over to Proverbs 9:1: *Wisdom has built her house, she has hewn out her seven pillars.*

Her house—this woman's house was built with wisdom. Have you ever thought about the symbolism of seven pillars?

Some scholars say seven pillars suggest her house is large. Perhaps a pavilion is attached. In this case, then, the implication is that a woman's outreach is broad.

Other renowned Bible scholars explain seven pillars indicate completeness and perfection,[57] a covenant number, expressing harmony and unity, "the signature of holiness and blessing, completeness and rest."[58]

Are you seeing the theme of perfection, harmony, blessing, and royalty?

To "hew" means to carve out, cut and shape into wood, stone, or another hard surface.[59] With wisdom women build, shape, and structure families, communities, and nations.

So, what are the seven pillars of wisdom?

The Bible provides insight.

Proverbs 1:2–5 tells us:

> *To know wisdom and instruction, to perceive the words of understanding, to receive the instruction of wisdom, justice, judgment, and equity; to give prudence to the simple, to the young man knowledge and discretion—a wise man will hear and increase learning, and a man of understanding will attain wise counsel.*

And Matthew 7:24–25 says:

> *Therefore whoever hears these sayings of Mine, and does them, I will liken him to a wise man who built his house on the rock: and the rain descended, the floods came, and the winds blew and beat on that house; and it did not fall, for it was founded on the rock.*

Then James 3:17 states:

> *But the wisdom that is from above is first pure, then peaceable, gentle, willing to yield, full of mercy and good fruits, without partiality and without hypocrisy.*

Based on these scripture passages, scholars agree the seven pillars of wisdom are:

- Fear of God
- Knowledge
- Understanding
- Instruction
- Discretion
- Counsel and reproof

- Purity

Pure motives and a peaceable, gentle spirit allow us to produce fruit as evidence of godly wisdom.

Let's revisit Queen Esther's actions. Based on the previous Scriptures, we could rename her "Wise Esther."

ESTHER	DEMONSTRATED
Esther fasted and prayed.	Faith and Reverence
Esther, although in a powerful position of authority, took others into consideration.	Understanding
Esther devised and implemented a plan.	Knowledge
Esther considered what was at stake.	Courage
Esther approached the king at the right time.	Discretion
Esther obeyed God and her counselors.	Love

Wisdom is the spiritual light guiding our thought process and consequent actions in all areas. Do any of these resonate?

- Finding boundaries with adult children
- Balancing activities
- Seeking medical treatment
- Sharing the gospel
- Maintaining productivity
- Cultivating and dissolving relationships
- Fulfilling your purpose
- Caring for an elderly parent
- Managing conflict
- Giving or seeking forgiveness
- Pursuing marital advice
- Striving toward financial freedom
- Investigating career options

Basically, we need wisdom in all areas of life. In what areas do you currently need wisdom?

During our third week, we'll talk about how godly wisdom enables us to take our position as a pillar.

Day 1: Fear That Shines

Day 2: Knowledge and Understanding That Enlighten

Day 3: Confrontation, Correction, Counsel … *Oh My!*

Day 4: Brightened with Discernment

Day 5: The Evidence of Godly Wisdom

God loves us. He wants us to be wise.

Pray as you begin your five studies this week. Ask God to open your eyes to see, your mind to understand, and your ears to listen.

Week Three, Day 1

Fear That Shines

I cannot work; I cannot speak; I cannot live or love as I should, unless God's
wisdom lights my path.
Dr. David Jeremiah[60]

*I pray, LORD God of heaven, O great and awesome God, You who keep Your
covenant and mercy with those who love You and observe Your commandments,
please let Your ear be attentive and Your eyes open, that You may hear the prayer
of Your servant which I pray before You now, day and night, for the children of
Israel Your servants, and confess the sins of the children of Israel which we have
sinned against You. Both my father's house and I have sinned. We have acted very
corruptly against You, and have not kept the commandments, the statutes, nor the
ordinances which You commanded Your servant Moses. Remember, I pray, the
word that You commanded Your servant Moses, saying, 'If you are unfaithful, I
will scatter you among the nations; but if you return to Me, and keep My
commandments and do them, though some of you were cast out to the farthest
part of the heavens, yet I will gather them from there, and bring them to the place
which I have chosen as a dwelling for My name.'*
Nehemiah 1:5-9

Pivotal Point: Love and respect for God compels us to obedience.

A lot of people are afraid.

In a 2020—2021 poll, more than 51 percent of Americans said they feared cyber
terrorism, economic collapse, civil unrest, illness, and loved ones dying. Seventy-
nine percent of Americans reported that corrupt government officials was their
top fear.[61]

Persistent fear can lead to phobias, one of the most common mental illnesses in
the United States. In fact, more than 12 percent of adults will deal with a specific
phobia in their lifetime.[62]

This anxiety-producing fear, however, isn't the way we should respond to God.

Quite the opposite, in fact.

In *The Highest Good—the Pilgrim's Songbook,* Author Oswald Chambers wrote in his book, "The remarkable thing about fearing God is that, when you fear God, you fear nothing else; whereas, if you do not fear God, you fear everything else."[63]

Chambers statement is more than interesting. It brings the fear factor into question.

Hmm.

How should we respond to God? The Bible says this:

> The ***fear*** *of the* LORD *is the beginning of knowledge, but fools despise wisdom and instruction.* (Proverbs 1:7, emphasis mine)

> The ***fear*** *of the* LORD *is the beginning of wisdom, and the knowledge of the Holy One is understanding.* (Proverbs 9:10, emphasis mine)

> The ***fear*** *of the* LORD *is the instruction of wisdom, and before honor is humility.* (Proverbs 15:33, emphasis mine)

This fear doesn't cause anxiety. This fear produces wisdom.

Your answer to the following question may depend on how you were brought up, what part of the world you live in, how you have personally experienced God, or what you know about His character. What do you think it means to fear God?

In the context of our Proverb verses, fear is translated "awe"[64] and means respect, reverence, and worship.[65]

The right way to respond to God is with reverence.

Reverence and respect are demonstrated in how we live. Additionally, these attitudes are prerequisites to wisdom. And wisdom permits women to become strong and supportive pillars.

How does our culture show respect for God?

In what ways is our culture irreverent?

In what ways do you specifically demonstrate your respect of God?

Is there a disrespectful habit in your life? If yes, what is it?

When we study the Bible, we gain knowledge about God's character and who He is. And when we personally experience God's love, provision, and mercy in our lives, our faith grows. But so does our respect. And this respect helps us believe His words and promises.

Let's be diligent to remember why God is worthy. Let's start today.

Let's read this eye-opening passage together, found in Psalm 103:1–18. Think about these questions as you read this passage: Who is God? What does He do?

What attributes of our God are listed in verses 1–10?

No other god or person can do what our God does.

No other god or person can be who our God is.

No one is more worthy of our admiration, awe, and respect, than Almighty God. Not our spouse, children, boss, or friend. God alone perfectly proves His character.

Did you think it's strange to read *pity* in verse 13? Often, we use this word to indicate that we feel sorry for someone. But not here. In this context, pity comes from the Hebrew word *chanan* and means to be gracious and find favor.[66]

Game changer. God favors us. He favors *you!*

Glance back at verses 11 and 17, then fill in the blank:

Toward those who _______________________________*Him.*

What does fearing God compel us do? The answer is given in verse 18.

What is God speaking to your heart right now?

The passage in Luke 5:1–11 is simple, yet profound. It may be a familiar Bible story, or it could be brand new. The translation you use won't matter. You'll get the gist of it. I'll prompt you with leading questions so you can summarize the activity and response in each verse.

Where was Jesus? (v. 1)

What were the fisherman doing? (v. 2)

Whose boat did Jesus get into? What did He do? (v. 3)

What did Jesus tell Simon (also called Simon Peter) to do? (v. 4)

What did Simon explain? (v. 5) Which did he do at Jesus's command? (Circle one): disobey or obey. Why do you think Simon responded in this manner?

How many fish were caught? (v. 6)

How did the fishermen respond to the unexpected catch? (v. 7)

What did Simon do? What did he say? (v. 8)

How does this verse describe Simon's emotion? (v. 9)

How did Simon's partners, James and John, react? (v. 10)

How will their future be different? (v. 11)

Depending on the version of the Bible you're using, you may have read the words *astonished* (in the NIV and NKJV). The NASB uses the word *amazement.*

Amazed means wow!

In fact, *amazement* comes from the Greek word *thambos* meaning "utter amazement with a sense of wonder." [67]

Synonyms for amazement include astounded, blown away, flabbergasted, awestruck. I admit, sometimes I talk about a delicious dessert as tasting amazing or I was blown away by a particular speaker's message.

Am I amazed by God?

What about you? Are you as amazed as Simon Peter at what God is doing in and around you? How has God amazed you recently?

In the previous passage, humility, amazement, reverence, and respect led Simon Peter and the others to obey Jesus and follow Him.

The Bible says in John 14:15, *If you love Me, keep My commandments.*

These next few questions might be difficult. In fact, you may need to pray through these and ask God to help you answer honestly.

Do you love Jesus? If yes, in what ways do you demonstrate your love?

What is God calling you to do or start in this season of your life? In what ways will you show your obedience to Him?

Is there a habit God is calling you to stop? If yes, what is it?

What action steps will you take to obey Him?

Jesus is our perfect example. He tells the Pharisees in John 8:55, *I do know Him [God] and keep His word.*

Jesus obeyed.

We don't have to stress or panic at the word *obedience.* God remembers we were created from dust. It was never God's intention and plan for us to live separate from Him, focused on what the world values and sees as wisdom. He knows we need His wisdom only.

So, let's get connected. Let's seek Him—communicate with Him through prayer and spend time with Him. The people in the Bible who were plugged in to their relationship with God were successful. One such person, for example, was Moses. And the Bible records that his face radiated with light (Exodus 34:35).

When we plug in to the ultimate Power Source, we'll radiate too.

What specifically are you choosing to believe from God's Word today?

Day One's Sparkling Gem: I believe I am wise when I respect and obey God.

Prayer: Holy, holy, holy, are You, God. You are the One true God. There is no other. No other person or statue can do what You do or know what You know. You are the first and the last, and You are in complete control. You are my Father, and I thank You for loving me so much. Thank You for making a way for me to spend eternity with You. It is my desire to respect the name of my precious Lord Jesus and sovereign God. In Jesus's name, amen.

Perspective: Make it your daily practice to worship God through music. Listen to, or sing with, songs proclaiming the holiness and majesty of God. The hymn "Holy, Holy, Holy" is a great one to begin with. Worshiping God creates an attitude of reverence.

Week Three, Day 2

Knowledge and Understanding That Enlighten

Wisdom is the right use of knowledge. To know is not to be wise. Many men know a great deal, and are all the greater fools for it. There is no fool so great a fool as a knowing fool. But to know how to use knowledge is to have wisdom.
Charles Spurgeon[68]

If you receive my words, and treasure my commands within you, so that you incline your ear to wisdom, and apply your heart to understanding; yes, if you cry out for discernment, and lift up your voice for understanding, if you seek her as silver, and search for her as for hidden treasures; then you will understand the fear of the LORD, And find the knowledge of God. For the LORD gives wisdom; from His mouth come knowledge and understanding.
Proverbs 2:1–6

Pivotal Point: Knowledge and understanding make good decision-making possible.

If you're of a certain age, you may recall Sergeant Joe Friday (played by Jack Webb) on the old 1951–1959 television show, *Dragnet*. To solve any crime, Sergeant Friday needed information, understanding, and knowledge about the case—the people, motives, and circumstances. His famous statement has lingered for decades: "All we want are the facts, ma'am." Some have shortened the phrase: "Just the facts, ma'am."

Do you, like Joe Friday, need facts?

We all want essential information, knowledge, and understanding to solve problems and make decisions.

Fortunately, we have access to God's perspective.

With approximately 1,440 minutes in a day, decision-making consumes much of our time. Do I want coffee or tea? Should I make an appointment during lunch break? Do I really want to take a call? Do I have time to respond to this text?

Many of the decisions we're making, though, aren't as simple. At some point, we all face life-changing decisions:

- Which school or childcare is the right choice?
- Should I buy this house?
- Should I take this job?
- Is it time to retire?
- What is the best treatment option for this illness or disease?
- What career path should I choose?
- How involved should I be in my adult children's lives?
- When do I say yes? Or no?

Before we make a decision, it's wise to research the topic and get the facts. You know, find out more of what's required or what the repercussions may be.

Reflect on these two questions for a few minutes: What major decision are you facing? For what issue do you need answers?

Just the facts, God, just give me the facts. Clearly tell me what to do.

My friend, Grace (name changed), shares her story:

> Red welts and a mysterious rash blanketed my body and burned like a sunburn. Often these cuts cracked open and bled, leaving me in constant pain. The rash on the bottoms of my feet made it difficult to walk.
>
> Along with the soreness, pain, cuts, boils, and redness, my skin was peeling—chunks as big as an inch. When I awoke each morning, my bed looked to be covered in rice—the smaller flakes.
>
> My face looked … well, like someone had drawn a clown face on me. Red circles framed my eyes; the circumference of my mouth was red, swollen and cracked. I couldn't open my mouth wide enough to insert food, so I lived on smoothies. I was actually thrilled to wear a mask during the COVID-19 pandemic. I could hide. And others couldn't see what I saw in the mirror.
>
> Over a two-year period, I sought help from twenty doctors and specialists, including homoeopathic and natural doctors.
>
> "You're the unicorn patient," they said. "You're unique and don't fit any profile for disease."

I endured numerous tests, four skin biopsies, and several other unpleasant procedures. For temporary pain relief, I used pain medication, oral steroids and topicals.

Then I finally had enough. One early morning in the quiet of my home, I fell down on my cracked knees and called out to God.

"God, what's causing this?"

I pleaded in desperation for days, asking Him to show me what to do.

Several days later a random thought popped into my head while looking at my red, swollen mouth. *Could it be something I'm eating?*

I began a cleanse (a fast) while going through the pantry and refrigerator looking for products with a common denominator ingredient.

I found a few and eliminated them one by one. Within a short period of time, I identified my allergy, tested the theory, and to my astonishment, it worked!

First my face cleared, then the rest of my body followed suit.

Today, I've happily removed the mask, scarves, hats, gloves, and long pants I used to cover up with. I am now enjoying summer weather with clear skin.

God gave me the knowledge—a thought to check food ingredients. I found relief and my life has been changed!

Grace observed (gained knowledge), applied the knowledge (wisdom), then benefitted (learned a lesson—she had a food allergy).

Grace did what Proverbs 24:32 says: *I applied my heart to what I observed and learned a lesson from what I saw* (NIV).

Her story reminded me of a statement Henry T. Blackaby wrote in *Experiencing God*:

> God doesn't want people to do what they think is best: He wants them to do what He knows is best, and no amount of reasoning and intellectualizing will discover that.[69]

Reflect. How did Grace make the leap from depending only on what was seen to the unseen? What was the outcome?

Amazing, isn't it? God's wisdom is within our grasp. Take a look at one of the many passages where God gives explicit direction. Read Isaiah 28:23–26:

> *Give ear and hear my voice, listen and hear my speech. Does the plowman keep plowing all day to sow? Does he keep turning his soil and breaking the clods? When he has leveled its surface, does he not sow the black cummin and scatter the cummin, plant the wheat in rows, the barley in the appointed place, and the spelt in its place? For He instructs him in right judgment, His God teaches him.*

How did the farmer learn to plow and plant effectively?

Both Grace and the farmer applied the knowledge God gave them and wisely implemented the plan.

For clarification, having *only* knowledge isn't the same as having wisdom. Knowledge is "information gained through experience, reasoning, or acquaintance." Wisdom is "the ability to discern or judge what is true, right, or lasting."[70]

The Greek word for wisdom is *sophia.* Having knowledge doesn't make us wise. Learning from experiences and benefiting from our challenges makes one wise.[71]

Author and Bible commentator Warren Wiersbe, helps put this in perspective: "Knowledge enables us to take things apart, but wisdom enables us to put things together and relate truth to daily life."[72]

Get the facts. Get understanding. Get knowledge. Using these tools in the right way produces wisdom and leads to success.

Let's return to a question asked earlier. What do you need to know about? The Bible provides powerful verses we can turn into our prayers. For example, we can say to God:

> You said, *Your ears shall hear a word behind you, "This is the way, walk in it," whenever you turn to the right hand or to the left* (Isaiah 30:21).

> You said, *I will instruct you and teach you in the way you should go; I will counsel you with my loving eye on you* (Psalm 32:8 NIV).

> You said, *Call to me, and I will answer you, and show you great and mighty things, you do not know* (Jeremiah 33:3).

> You said, *I will make each of My mountains a road, And My highways shall be elevated* (Isaiah 49:11).

> You said, *Trust in the Lord with all your heart and lean not on your own understanding; in all your ways submit to Him, and He will make your paths straight* (Proverbs 3:5–6 NIV).

Refer to the previous verse. Circle *"lean not on your own understanding."* Put a box around *"submit to Him, and He will make your paths straight."* What parts are our responsibility? Which part is God's?

Continue praying, *Show me Your ways, Lord, teach me Your paths. Guide me in Your truth and teach me, for You are God my Savior, and my hope is in You all day long* (Psalm 25:4–5 NIV).

God desires to illuminate our darkness and shine the light on the right path. Then we will be as *Those who are wise will shine like the brightness of the heavens, and those who lead many to righteousness, like the stars for ever and ever* (Daniel 12:3 NIV).

Shine on . . . you're a star!

What specifically are you choosing to believe from God's Word today?

Day Two's Sparkling Gem: I believe God provides me with knowledge to make sound decisions.

Prayer: Wise Father, Thank You for loving me so much. Your desire is to make me wise in all areas. There's nothing I can't bring to You. Every decision and problem is one You want to help me with. Today I ask specifically for wisdom with ___________________. Thank you, God. In Jesus's name, amen.

Perspective: Paint stars with gold glitter paint pens and attach them to a black backdrop—foam or construction paper or tag board works well. With a white or yellow maker, write Daniel 12:3 across the top: *Those who are wise will shine like the brightness of the heavens.*

Week Three, Day 3

Confrontation, Correction, Counsel … *Oh My!*

If you lack knowledge, go to school. If you lack wisdom, get on your knees!
Knowledge is not wisdom. Wisdom is the proper use of knowledge.
Vance Havner[73]

*If your brother or sister sins, go and point out their fault, just between the two of
you. If they listen to you, you have won them over. But if they will not listen, take
one or two others along, so that every matter may be established by the testimony
of two or three witnesses. If they still refuse to listen, tell it to the church; and if
they refuse to listen even to the church, treat them as you would a pagan or a tax
collector.*

Matthew 18:15–17

Pivotal Point: Confrontation, correction, and counsel build wisdom.

"What do you think wisdom is?"

As a regular substitute teacher in a fourth-grade class, I had come to expect
Mason's deep thinking. Still his answer took me by surprise one day.

"Wisdom," he said, "comes from your experience in the world and how you use it
to impact people in good ways."

He must have noticed my surprise because he gave me a sheepish grin.

I tore out a sheet of paper from a notebook.

"Write those words down."

I wanted to remember that moment. He was glad to oblige. (Today I still have
Mason's note!)

Mason's definition is similar to those of Bible scholars we've already discussed.

From morning till night, we have a multitude of experiences.

Think about the sweet moments and wonderful successes over the past week or
month or year.

Then there are surprising defeats, inevitable consequences, crushing heartbreak, and more.

Which came to your mind first—the sweet moments or the defeats? It really doesn't matter. Every day is an opportunity to gain experience, grow in wisdom, learn from our mistakes, and repeat our strategies for success.

The Bible teaches us how to be wise, specifically in the area of confrontation, correction, and counsel:

> *Reproofs of instruction are the way of life.* (Proverbs 6:23)

> *He who keeps instruction is in the way of life, but he who refuses correction goes astray.* (Proverbs 10:17)

> *The way of a fool is right in his own eyes, but he who heeds counsel is wise.* (Proverbs 12:15)

> *Without counsel, plans go awry, but in the multitude of counselors they are established.* (Proverbs 15:22)

> *The ear that hears the rebukes of life will abide among the wise.* (Proverbs 15:31)

> *Listen to counsel and receive instruction, that you may be wise in your latter days.* (Proverbs 19:20)

How would you summarize the previous verses? Is there a theme? What are the frequently used words or ideas?

Let's not be offended by this next verse. Or … let's!

None of us want to be labeled as stupid. But Proverbs 12:1 tells us, *Whoever loves instruction loves knowledge, but he who hates correction is stupid.*

Resist stupidity. Receiving correction is wise.

For starters, where do you turn for counsel? Circle all that apply:

All friends	Pastors	Fortune Teller	Prayer
Godly friends	Bible	Professional counselor	Newspaper
Horoscope	Family Member	Secular Books	Other __________

Sometimes we seek out correction for ourselves; other times, we bring it. The Bible teaches us how to take action. Second Timothy 3:16 says, *All Scripture is given by inspiration of God, and is profitable for doctrine, for reproof, for correction, for instruction in righteousness.*

Read 2 Timothy 4:2. Depending on the translation you're using you may have read:

Preach the word; be ready in season and out of season . . . reprove, rebuke, exhort, with great patience and instruction. (NASB, KJV)

. . . correct, rebuke and encourage–with great patience and careful instruction. (NIV)

. . . reprove, rebuke, and exhort, with complete patience and teaching. (ESV)

. . . convince, rebuke, exhort, with all longsuffering and teaching. (NKJV)

. . . correct, confront, and encourage with patience and instruction, (CEB)

Most versions use *rebuke* in place of *correction*, and one uses the verb *confront*.

Barnes' Notes on the Bible clarifies the meaning of *rebuke*: "In the New Testament the word is used to express a judgment of what is wrong or contrary to one's will, and hence, to admonish or reprove. That word also implies no superior authority in him who does it. He presents 'reasons, or argues' the case, for the purpose of convincing."[74]

Similarly, the *Jamison Bible Commentary* defines reprove as [to] "convict, confute."[75]

Whether we use rebuke, confront, oppose, or reprove, 2 Timothy 4:2 says to approach a person with encouragement, patience, instruction, or teaching.

To simplify the repetitive phrase of *confrontation, correction, and counsel,* I'll refer to these three words as the 3 C's.

The 3 C's can dredge up anger, embarrassment, and defensiveness. Confrontation in particular may be uncomfortable for one or both parties. You may wonder, Will it start a quarrel? Is it too abrasive? Will it damage the relationship? Will the person whom I'm confronting think I believe I'm superior?

First, let's establish what confrontation means. Then we'll look at five biblical strategies to help us when confrontation is necessary.

From a secular perspective, confrontation implies hostility and can involve a clash of words or physical violence. Nowadays, the word often refers to a military encounter involving opposing armies. This meaning became popular after the Cuban Missile Crisis in 1963. Before that, confrontation was used to mean "bringing two opposing parties face to face."[76]

Are you comfortable with confrontation, or do you choose to avoid it?

Following are five biblical strategies for dealing with 3 C's:

    1.   Choose Words Carefully

Read 1 Timothy 4:13. Fill in the missing word:

Give attention to reading, to _______________________________, to doctrine.

Most translations use the word "exhortation". The Greek word translated *exhortation* means to "come alongside and help."[77] It involves comforting someone with strength and encouragement. Correction conveys the same idea. We come alongside a person to give counsel and show how the Scriptures relate to a situation.

In this way, how are encouragement and confrontation related?

Match each verse to its reference.

*There is one who speaks like the piercings of a sword, but the tongue of the wise promotes **health**.*	2 Timothy 2:25 (emphasis added)
*Brethren, if a man is overtaken in any trespass, you who are spiritual **restore** such a one in a spirit of gentleness, considering yourself lest you also be tempted.*	Proverbs 12:18 (emphasis added)
*In humility correct those who are in opposition, if God perhaps will grant them repentance, so that they may know the **truth.***	Galatians 6:1 (emphasis added)

What do these verses teach us about our attitude?

What is the intended purpose in a confrontation? (Hint: the answer is in bold print)

Galatians 6:1 says, *Lest you be tempted also?* What do you think this verse means? Tempted to do what?

Teachers think about the best way to help their students understand, and lawyers think about the best way to expose the truth. Likewise, let's think carefully about the words we use so they bring about understanding, reconciliation, and conviction.

2.   Love Must Be Our Motivation

Before we confront someone with correction, let's ask ourselves: Is my goal to promote spiritual health and reconciliation to God? Or is the reason to flaunt spiritual knowledge or appear superior?

The story of the Samaritan woman is found in John 4:7–42. Jesus's journeys were strategic. In this case, He met a woman at a well. He spoke to her kindly and gently convicted her of sin.

What was her reaction to His gentle rebuke (see verses 15, 25, 29, 39)?

Sometimes a more direct approach is needed, like when Jesus confronted the Pharisees for being hypocritical and judgmental (Matthew 23). Nicodemus was one of these Pharisees, yet after his confrontation with Jesus, he later believed Jesus was the Messiah. (See John 19)

I love His style!

Jesus's confrontation flowed from love and a genuine desire to help another person be restored. He never used confrontation as a means of retaliation; neither was He motivated by an "I told you so" attitude.

3.   Are the 3 C's always the best approach?

Not always. When emotional or mental issues are present, correction may be misunderstood. The best option in those cases is prayer.

Second Timothy 2:23–24 tells us, *Avoid foolish and ignorant disputes, knowing that they generate strife. And a servant of the Lord must not quarrel but be gentle to all, able to teach, patient.*

When we confront someone in love with the intent of restoration, then confrontation isn't foolish. Rather, it's necessary for restoration or for the person's spiritual growth. From this perspective, confrontation, done properly, shows love.

Additionally, Jesus didn't address every wrong action or thought. When the soldiers came to arrest Him in the garden of Gethsemane, He didn't correct them or defend Himself (Matthew 26).

Once I was with a group of women from various Christian denominations. One woman criticized my denomination. She was snarky, and her comment was out of context. I asked God if I should confront her about her hurtful words and watered-down theology. I felt God leading me to stay quiet.

We don't have to argue every point, especially about personal preferences in worship or nonessentials of church practice. Neither she nor I ever brought up the incident again.

4.   Avoid Impulsivity and Invest Time in Prayer.

Seek godly wisdom. Ask God to prepare the person's heart and mind to receive your correction.

Ask God to give you the right words.

Ask God to help you both listen with the intent of understanding.

And remember, you're not in this alone. The Holy Spirit is with you and will help you speak: *When He, the Spirit of truth, has come, He will guide you into all truth* (John 16:13).

Do you need to have a conversation with someone? If so, write out a prayer now to help you begin praying for this person.

5.   Timing Is Important

If God gives the green light and opens the door for correction to take place, He will show you the opportune time. Meeting with a person after an extra-long, stressful day at work may not be the best time. Proverbs 27:14 tells us, *He who blesses his friend with a loud voice, rising early in the morning, it will be counted a curse to him.*

What do you think this verse implies?

Recall a 3 C's situation when bad timing made matters worse. Was the issue resolved? Why or why not?

Reflect on a time when a godly person brought the 3 C's to you in truth and love. How was that conversation beneficial? How were you protected? In other words, when you learned the danger of a potential situation, attitude, or sin, how did that change you?

Finally, don't be consumed with how a person responds. Their response is between them and God.

We can apply these same five strategies when someone needs to correct us. Correction makes us wise and illuminates our understanding when we allow God to humble our hearts to receive it.

What specifically are you choosing to believe from God's Word today?

Day Three's Sparkling Gem: I believe God's wisdom and direction will guide me when confrontation, counsel, or correction is necessary.

Prayer: Father, thank You for Your wisdom and direction. Help me know how and when and if I should confront ___________________________ about a situation. Give me words. Prepare this person's heart and mind. In Jesus's name, amen.

Perspective: Using colorful construction paper or decorative scrapbooking paper, cut a rectangle to the size you like for a bookmark. (I use roughly a 2 x 6 piece.) Then make a hole at the top with a hole puncher. Next, thread a ribbon through the hole. Write the five things to do before you confront, counsel, or correct another person. Keep it in your purse or Bible and refer to it when needed.

Week Three, Day 4

Brightened with Discernment

Discernment is not the ability to tell the difference between right and wrong;
rather, it is telling the difference between right and almost right.
Charles Spurgeon[78]

*Let no one deceive you with empty words, for because of these things the wrath of
God comes upon the sons of disobedience. Therefore do not become partners with
them; for at one time you were darkness, but now you are light in the Lord. Walk
as children of light (for the fruit of light is found in all that is good and right and
true), and try to discern what is pleasing to the Lord.*
Ephesians 5:6–10

Pivotal Point: Wisdom and discernment illuminate God's will.

I sat on the balcony of my daughter and sons-in-law's rented condominium. It was
sweltering hot on Hilton Head Island. Although I was shaded, sweat cascaded
down my face and onto my papers—my journal, notes, and Bible. Sweat mingled
with tears, to put it more accurately. I opened my prayer journal to re-read my
own words: "God, grow me in wisdom, knowledge, understanding, and
discretion."

Tears flow more easily these days since my husband, Alan, died from cancer only
six months ago. Problem-solving, praying, investing, and decision-making were
things we did together. Now I'm alone. Or so it seemed.

I've been thrust into making decisions, many of them financial, all by myself.
Alan was my best friend and confidant. It's not about *needing* his help; the truth is
I *preferred* making decisions with him. Without him, what's ahead is unclear,
confusing, and even dark. I need discernment.

As the sun moved across the sky that day, God's light pierced my heart. The Holy
Spirit brought Psalm 20:7 to my mind: *Some trust in chariots, and some in
horses; but we will remember the name of the LORD our God.*

God illuminated my darkness with deep, insightful truth.

For sure, some people trust in their financial advisors, bankers, attorneys, doctors,
counselors, or accountants. God often uses these professionals to help guide us.

Others make decisions based on advice from the government or an international committee. The point is, though, no person or institution can know, predict, or guess what our supreme God knows with certainty.

Since God is the source of all wisdom, understanding, knowledge and discretion, He is enough. Let's diligently seek Him, pay attention to what He reveals, apply the lessons from previous experiences, and walk in obedience. In this way, we build our houses with pillars of wisdom.

Psalm 127:1 tells us, *Unless the Lord builds the house, the builders labor in vain. Unless the Lord watches over the city, the guards stand watch in vain.*

Today we'll study a woman whose husband was a fool. There's not a great deal written in the Bible about Abigail, but what has been written is significant: *She was a woman of good understanding, and of a beautiful countenance* (1 Samuel 25:3).

Two other translations put it this way:

> *The woman was discerning and beautiful.* (ESV)

> *The woman was intelligent and beautiful in appearance.* (NASB)

Abigail—understanding, discerning, intelligent, and beautiful—similar qualities to our gal, Esther.

For clarification, to *discern* is to have the ability to see, recognize, or understand something that is not clear.[79] Another dictionary defines discernment like this: "the trait of judging wisely and objectively."[80]

Synonyms for discernment include discretion, perceptiveness, judgment, wisdom, understanding, and insight. But these words are much more than merely synonyms.

Colossians 2:3 identifies wisdom and knowledge as treasures, far more valuable than what the world has to offer. God shatters the darkness of society's temporary, faulty, opinion and extends to us His treasure—His eternal, infallible wisdom. Do we crave life-preserving treasure, or do we settle for that which is worthless?

Abigail's triumphant story unfolds in 1 Samuel 25. I'll summarize this chapter:

> Abigail was married to Nabal—a rich, arrogant, selfish, foolish,
> evil man. King David and his 600 warriors stayed clear of Nabal's
> livestock, enabling him to profit even more. Sometime later, David
> sent ten men to ask for provisions from Nabal. He scoffed and
> refused, even mocking David. This angered David, who now
> wanted vengeance. Sensing danger, one of Nabal's men spoke to
> Abigail, and begged her to use her influence and intervene. She
> didn't tell her husband, and she didn't waste any time.
>
> She assembled a caravan of donkeys with provisions for David and
> his men—200 fresh loaves of bread, two skins of wine, roasted
> grain, 100 cakes of raisins, and 200 cakes of pressed figs, and
> dressed sheep, skinned and ready to be cooked. What a feast!
> When Abigail saw David, she apologized for her husband's foolish
> behavior. She told David, "God would be the One to avenge." She
> encouraged him for his righteousness and spoke a blessing over
> him.

Allow me to paraphrase David's response: "I'm so glad you spoke up! You saved
me from sin and seeking vengeance."

> After her encounter, Abigail returned to Nabal. He was drunk
> again and acting foolishly. She waited till morning, then
> courageously told her husband what she had done. The anger and
> shock must have been too much. His heart failed and ten days later,
> he died.

We don't know everything Abigail must have put up with in her marriage to a
selfish, evil man, but we can read between the lines enough to know it must have
been difficult for her. And yet …

G O, A-B-I-G-A-I-L (G O, E-S-T-H-E-R)

I feel like a cheerleader chanting the victory call. These women were both
positioned at the right time to fulfill God's will.

Mordecai called on Esther to intervene. Who approached Abigail? What was his
request?

Neither Esther nor Abigail wasted time in creating a plan of action. What was Abigail's plan?

How did Abigail approach David? What were her posture, attitude, and words?

What comparisons can you draw between the actions of these two women?

What attributes do Esther and Abigail share?

Esther and Abigail were both married to wealthy, powerful men. Yet, God used the bold (and risky) acts of these women—their wives—to fulfill His purpose.

The following verses can become our personal prayers. Match the verse and reference.

1 Kings 3:9	*I am your servant; give me discernment that I may understand your statutes.*
Psalm 112:5	*Dear friends, do not believe every spirit, but test the spirits to see whether they are from God, because many false prophets have gone out into the world.*
Psalm 119:125	*The rich are wise in their own eyes; one who is poor and discerning sees how deluded they are.*

Proverbs 15:14	*Folly brings joy to one who has no sense, but whoever has understanding keeps a straight course.*
Proverbs 15:21	*And this I pray, that your love may abound still more and more in knowledge and all discernment, that you may approve the things that are excellent, that you may be sincere and without offense till the day of Christ.*
Proverbs 18:15	*So give your servant a discerning heart to govern your people and to distinguish between right and wrong. For who is able to govern this great people of yours?*
Proverbs 28:11	*The heart of the discerning acquires knowledge, for the ears of the wise seek it out.*
Philippians 1:9–10	*A good man deals graciously and lends; he will guide his affairs with discretion.*
1 John 4:1	*The discerning heart seeks knowledge, but the mouth of a fool feeds on folly.*

We read Solomon's simple yet profound words in Proverbs 2:1–5 in our previous lesson, but let's review them:

> *My son, if you receive my words, and treasure my commands within you, so that you incline your ear to wisdom, and apply your heart to understanding; yes, if you cry out for discernment, and lift up your voice for understanding, if you seek her as silver, and search for her as for hidden treasures; then you will understand the fear of the Lord, and find the knowledge of God.*

As in the game show *Jeopardy,* we have the answer spelled out in the previous passage. The question is, "What are we doing to receive it?" Let's revisit these statements written on the previous pages and make them your own.

In what ways do you seek God?

How do you receive, take in, absorb God's words?

How does God generally speak to you?

When God nudges you or opens your eyes to ideas or new opportunities, in what ways do you apply His leading?

What steps do you need to take to walk in obedience?

Do you ask God specifically for wisdom? If yes, what have you learned? If no, do you better understand the power your prayer can release now?

In what ways do you seek discernment and understanding? Do you seek it more than you seek the treasures on earth? If no, what's holding you back?

Pursue discernment. Seek His treasures. Exchange darkness and fear for wisdom to become a pillar and a *light of the world. A city that is set on a hill cannot be hidden* (Matthew 5:14).

What specifically are you choosing to believe from God's Word today?

Day Four's Sparkling Gem: I believe discernment helps me determine the best plan of action.

Prayer: Almighty Father, thank You that it is Your delight to give us with wisdom and discernment so we can establish good relationships, work ethics, and make sound decisions that affect all areas of our life. I ask you now to give me wisdom for this day so I can stand boldly as the pillar you designed me to be. In Jesus's name, amen.

Perspective: For your early morning or late-night quiet times, purchase a lantern that contains a battery-operated candle inside. Turn on the light to brighten the space and remind you that you are a light for the world.

Week Three, Day 5

The Evidence

The fruit of the Spirit working through millions of believers by faith could literally change the world.
Dr. Bill Bright[81]

But also for this very reason, giving all diligence, add to your faith virtue, to virtue knowledge, to knowledge self-control, to self-control, perseverance, to perseverance godliness, to godliness brotherly kindness, and to brotherly kindness love. For if these things are yours and abound, you will be neither barren nor unfruitful in the knowledge of our Lord Jesus Christ.
2 Peter 1:5–8

Pivotal Point: Worldly or divine Wisdom is evident in our lives.

A life lesson occurred twenty-five years ago when five-year-old Will, covered in a mixture of chocolate ice cream and dirt, ran into the house screaming with excitement.

"Mom, Dad, I found a bird egg!" he proudly declared. "It's white with bluish-gray speckles."

After chatting about God's creation, my husband and I explained the egg needed to go back in the nest so its mother could take care of it. Will left to return the egg to its nest. Within moments, however, he came back into the kitchen.

"Mom, I didn't get to put the egg back." His mouth hung open in surprise. "I don't know what happened. I put the egg in my pocket and then . . . something strange happened . . . and there's a baby bird!" he finally said.

Will and his dad settled the baby bird back into its nest right away.

Later, I found Will's pants on the washing machine. I pulled the pocket inside out and there it was—evidence of new life beginning. Fragments of eggshells and blood filled the pocket lining. Alone in the dimly lit laundry room, I stood silent. If I hadn't seen the evidence, I wouldn't have believed it. New life actually began in my son's pants pocket.

God eclipsed my thoughts with His when He gently spoke to my heart.

What about you? Is there evidence you have new life in Me?[82]

The experience was a life-changing moment for me. A deep, convicting spiritual lesson.

Evidence surrounds us.

Evidence left at a crime scene aids the detective's investigation.

Proof of a new season is evident when ice crystals glisten on tree limbs.

Shaking tree leaves confirm the wind is blowing.

A smile testifies to the feeling of delight.

What we believe about God and the choices we make are also evidence of our faith.

A woman's actions prove what she believes about God, her identity in Him, His purpose for her, and her mission on earth.

Recall what the apostle Paul says is evidence of God's wisdom in our life. Read Galatians 5:22–23 and list the fruit of the Spirit on the following lines:

_______________________   _______________________   _______________________

_______________________   _______________________   _______________________

_______________________   _______________________   _______________________

What a massive list!

I once prayed this prayer: You know I love You God and I want Your wisdom and the evidence of the Holy Spirit's work in me. I will exemplify fruit . . . and hopefully by tonight!

But acquiring fruit doesn't happen overnight.

Forcing a certain mindset or godly trait could lead to striving, temporary satisfaction, false humility, and hypocrisy.

But when we seek God though through Bible reading and prayer, the fruit of the Spirit emerges naturally.

Of the nine fruit you listed which one(s) is easiest for you?

In elementary school, one year I was given a *C* in Conduct. Yep, I talked too much. At the time the grade embarrassed me, but in retrospect I wasn't a bad kid. Rather, I was a child who lacked self-control. Talking isn't immoral in and of itself. But wisdom directs us to know when to speak, when to be quiet, and when to listen.

Which of the fruit of the Spirit is a challenge for you?

James 3:13–18 provides further explanation of good conduct and wisdom:

> *Who is wise and understanding among you? Let him show by good conduct that his works are done in the meekness of wisdom. But if you have bitter envy and self-seeking in your hearts, do not boast and lie against the truth. This wisdom does not descend from above, but is earthly, sensual, demonic. For where envy and self-seeking exist, confusion and every evil thing are there. For wisdom that is from above is first pure, then peaceable, gentle, willing to yield, full of mercy and good fruits, without partiality and without hypocrisy Now the fruit of righteousness is sown in peace by those who make peace.*

Based on this passage, how does the wisdom of God compare to earthly wisdom?

How do you think a woman becomes spiritually mature and wise?

If an older woman chooses to leave God out of her daily life, she remains unchanged by Him. A younger woman, however, who spends time in the Word of God, finds truth and wisdom. She is able to produce Christlike conduct—the fruit of the Spirit—because of the indwelling Holy Spirit.

Birthdays don't make us wise; following God does.

First Corinthians 1:25 says the world's wisdom is foolishness to God. Bible commentator Warren Wiersbe, compares the earth's wisdom to God's wisdom in this adapted chart:[83]

The World's Wisdom	God's Wisdom
Envious; self-promoting; selfish	Motivated to point others to God and show His glory
Striving; peer approval seeking; competitive; divisive	Humility; esteems others
Hypocritical; insincere; pretentious; deceitful	Open; honest
Boastful; proud	Resists urge to compare oneself to others
Deceitful	Truth-seeking; darkness exposing
Assertive in a self-seeking way	Self-controlled; God-honoring; wisdom-seeking
Worldly; sinful; spiritual unfaithful to God	Pure and holy because God is holy

Competitive; demanding; deceitful to hide sin	Peace; pure; confesses sin
Blaming; contentious; aggravating causes	Reasonable; truthful; gentle
Wavers; two-faced; fearful	Unchanging; single minded; decisive; strong; courageous
Hard to get along with; stubborn	Agreeable; easy to live and work with
Merciless; gives others "what they deserve;" hard-hearted	Merciful
Striving; chasing after the wind	Faithful, full life; practical; good works producing; abundant life

Which, if any, characteristics of man's wisdom is creating strife in your life?

How would you summarize the difference between God's wisdom and man's wisdom?

What this world offers leads to dissatisfaction, defeat, and death. But revering God brings a victorious life on earth and eternal life in heaven.

How have you been challenged in a specific area this week? How will you apply God's wisdom to your daily routine?

In what ways do you believe the lesson's opening statement—"The fruit of the Spirit working through millions of believers by faith could literally change the world"—is true?

Recall the elaborate staircase we opened with in Week Three's introduction. Go ahead, girl. Humbly and wisely run up. God is waiting for you!

What specifically are you choosing to believe from God's Word today?

Day Five's Sparkling Gem: I believe when I focus on God and seek His ways, His wisdom is evident in my life.

Prayer: Oh precious Father, I can confidently run to You to receive wisdom, knowledge, understanding, guidance, and strength to live a godly life. You alone are my help and all I need. When I seek You, I display evidence of Your wisdom. You are amazing, and my lips will praise You forever! Father, help me become a wise woman in all areas. I love You! In Jesus's name, amen.

Perspective: Find fruit magnets at your dollar or kitchen store. Using a permanent marker, write one fruit of the Spirit on each magnet. Place them on your refrigerator, file cabinet, or any other place to remind you of the beautiful evidence of Christ in your life.

Participant's Guide

Polished is removing the ______________________, the ______________________spots, smoothing out the ______________________ areas and dark texture.

In Psalm 69:1–2, David used the word ______________________to describe his pain.

The Greek word for perfection, *teleios*, means ______________________.

Various *trials* is translated in the KJV with the term ______________________.

Isaiah 43:2 is hope: *When you walk through the* ______________________ *you shall not be* ______________________ *nor shall the flame scorch you.*

Introduction: Week Four—She's Polished

View Introduction:
Week Four Video on YouTube:

Welcome back, strong, beautiful, wise woman!

You believe in God. But do you believe Him?

Believing God changes everything. In good seasons, we're thankful for His kindness.

When we're thrust into a terrifying trial, though, trusting and believing God becomes our hope and life.

Generally, when we trust someone, we follow their ideas and suggestions with ease.

Do you trust what God says in our key verse? Do you believe these words, this encouragement, this promise?

> *That our daughters may be as pillars, sculptured in palace style.*

Let's refresh. Consider Scripture's description of daughters as pillars in several translations.

- *Our daughters may be as pillars, sculptured in palace style.* (NKJV, emphasis mine, and following)
- *Our daughters may be as corner stones, polished after the similitude of a palace.* (KJV)
- *Our daughters will be like pillars carved to adorn a palace.* (NIV)
- When ... *our daughters [are] like corner pillars fashioned for a palace.* (NASB)

How lovely. How praiseworthy.

Each translation refers to a palace. What does this tell us about what God has in mind for His daughters and their place in His kingdom? What can we become with God's help?

Further commentary says this about Psalm 144:12:

> "The comparison is a very beautiful one, having the idea of grace …
> the skill of the sculptor is most abundantly lavished."[84]

> "Strong and beautiful, and adorned with all the ornaments belonging to
> their [gender]."[85]

> "Daughters—prudent, virtuous, healthful, industrious, and amiable …
> polished cornerstones both beautify and connect together the parts of a
> magnificent structure."[86]

> "Daughters unite families as cornerstones join walls together, and at
> the same time they adorn them as polished stones garnish the structure
> into which they are built. Home becomes a palace when the daughters
> are maids of honor, and the sons are nobles in spirit."[87]

Polished: removing the grit, the dark spots, smoothing out the rough areas and
dark texture. By definition, *polished* is something or someone who is:

- made smooth
- characterized by a high degree of development … or refinement, free from
  imperfections, or
- characterized by elegance and refinement.[88]

Do we have rough areas in our life to smooth? Do we sometimes feel like
someone is cutting us during a painful season?

One way a woman can become polished—shiny and refined—is by taking in
God's Word, adjusting herself to it, and living it out. This may include being
subjected to a painful chiseling process.

When I'm suffering or going through a challenging season, I say I'm in a trial.

Or darkness.

Or a storm.

Or maybe a fire.

In Psalm 69:1–2, David used the word *mire* to describe his pain.

What word do you use most often to define your pain?

The onset of a trial may surprise us, but we shouldn't be surprised. James 1:2–4 tells us:

> *My brethren, count it all joy when you fall into various trials, knowing that the testing of your faith produces, patience. But let patience have its perfect work, that you may be perfect and complete, lacking nothing.*

When. *Not* if.

Knowing trials are inevitable doesn't make me like them any better. However, within this passage we find purpose for trials: to make us perfect and complete.

The Greek word for perfection, *teleios*, means "completeness."[89]

Perfect faith in God makes us spiritually mature. To complete the process we'll need endurance. Romans 5:3–4 tells us:

> *But we also glory in tribulations, knowing that tribulation produces perseverance; and perseverance, character; and character, hope.*

Christ-followers gain additional endurance with each trial, which produces a deeper, stronger level of faith. Endurance is increased when we trust God for a good outcome.

And 2 Corinthians 4:17–18 tells us:

> *For our light affliction, which is but for a moment, is working for us a far more exceeding and eternal weight of glory, while we do not look at the things which are seen, but at the things which are not seen. For the things which are seen are temporary, but the things which are not seen are eternal.*

Now, these passages encourage me and give me hope.

Before we dive deeper, though, in the James 1:2–4 passage, *various trials* is translated in the KJV with the term divers temptation which means various temptations, those coming from the devil as he tempts us to do what we think will bring us pleasure, and those coming from our selfishness and ignorance. We can be tempted to worry, to fear, or to doubt God's love—definitely not pleasurable experiences.

You, too?

God never tempts us to sin. But because He loves us so much, He will allow testing for the purpose of transformation and refinement. His tests reveal what is in our own hearts, and His Word tells us what is good and what we can do about the rough spots.

Don't be disheartened, though. God is on our side and will help us. Job 23:10 tells us, *He knows the way that I take; when He has tested me, I will come forth as gold.*

And 1 Peter 1:7 adds, *The genuineness of your faith, being much more precious than gold that perishes, though it is tested by fire, may be found to praise, honor, and glory at the revelation of Jesus Christ.*

The refining process is unique for each of us, but we all feel the burn.

Did you know three New Testament Greek words are used for trial?

Check these out:

- *Purosis* alludes to going through the fires of suffering for the purpose of refining one's character.[90]
- *Perirasmos* implies God is testing our commitment. Will we remain faithful to Him, or will we give in to temptation and sin? [91]
- *Dokimion* refers to the refiner's fire and proves one's faith is genuine. After being tested, faith remains.[92]

Hey, I get it. We don't have to know these Greek words for trial to know that trials are painful. What's helpful, though, is knowing there is a reason and a purpose for our suffering. And if there's a common thread among us, it's that sometimes we're in the fires of adversity.

I can't fathom what Job went through. (Read his story in the book of Job chapters one and two, and forty-two.) Yet, through his suffering and great loss, he became spiritually mature and remained faithful to God.

And then there's Abraham. He waited years for Sarah to conceive a child. During those days of waiting and conflict, Abraham's faith was strengthened. Then later, when God asked for what we'd consider to be the unthinkable—to sacrifice his son—Abraham trusted God and obeyed. And he then worshipped when his son was spared.

We can't talk about trials and suffering and strong faith without mentioning King David. Known as "the man after God's heart," David describes his darkness in Psalm 32.

David refused to confess his sin with Bathsheba (See 2 Samuel 11–12). For an entire year, his guilt and shame were like a heaviness pressing upon his shoulders.

He writes that his *vitality was turned into the drought of summer* (v.4).

For clarification, *vitality* means "the capacity for survival or for the continuation of a meaningful or purposeful existence." [93]

Wow. A seriously dark time in David's life.

Lively character? Gone.

Mental vigor? Absent.

Active? Not much.

But God.

Don't you just love saying and reading those two precious words?

For one purpose or many, God used David's, Abraham's, and Job's trials to help them grow in perseverance, endurance, spiritual maturity, transformation, and refinement. And He does the same for us.

And always for His glory—which points us and others to Himself.

Isaiah 43:2 is hope: *When you walk through the fire, you shall not be burned, nor shall the flame scorch you.*

Oh, may we train our hearts to see God in our trials.

Our gal Esther spent one year in preparation before she was complete and equipped to go before the king.

We can't speculate on everything Esther endured. But we know the oil and spices absorbed into her body and produced a lovely fragrance. What a beautiful picture of what God is accomplishing in us. Like Esther, we'll undergo a beauty treatment, that produces a pleasing aroma to God. Recall 2 Corinthians 2:15: *For*

God's polishing:

- Prepares us for what we're headed into
- Purges the impurities of our heart
- Strengthens us for action
- Enables us to let go of the baggage weighing heavily upon our hearts
- Makes us shine so others are drawn to Him
- Teaches us to trust Him

Viewing the polishing process through this lens helps us submit. We can anticipate a marvelous outcome.

During our fourth week, we'll talk about the Refiner, the fires of refinement, and the victory to follow.

<table>
<tr><td>Day 1: The Refiner</td></tr>
<tr><td>Day 2: Stay Anchored</td></tr>
<tr><td>Day 3: Genuine Joy</td></tr>
<tr><td>Day 4: You're Grounded</td></tr>
<tr><td>Day 5: Remaining Faithful</td></tr>
</table>

Lord, I believe; help my unbelief! (Mark 9:24)

And as God helped Esther, He'll help us meet adversity with courage and boldness.

Week Four, Day 1

Our Refiner

Of one thing I am perfectly sure: God's story never ends with ashes.
Elisabeth Elliot[94]

"I will bring the one-third through the fire, will refine them as silver is refined, and test them as gold is tested. They will call on My name, and I will answer them. I will say, 'This is My people'; and each one will say, 'The LORD is my God.'"

Zechariah 13:9

Pivotal Point: Our lives are refined in the fires of affliction.

Last summer I built a small fire pit in my back yard. Measuring 5 feet by 5 feet, I laid landscape timbers to create a border. Next, I arranged concrete blocks in a circle. In the space between the border and the concrete blocks, I poured bags of large white rocks. The sticks that had blown from the trees and now rested around my yard made excellent kindling. When I strike a match to the sticks, within a few minutes a fire glows.

Flames and crackles are warm and delightful.

But flames are also powerful. Consuming. Destructive.

I was reminded of this fact months ago when I viewed some charred trees on a hike. I vividly recalled the sound of the fire engine sirens. Black smoke had impaired my view of the mountain ridge. When the smoke finally cleared and the fire was extinguished, I saw where the flames had licked the mountain ridge trees, stripping them of life.

Months later, when I returned to the mountain hiking trail, I stood amidst charred trees. I moved closer to touch an evergreen and I saw it—a tiny sprout of new life. A single, fresh branch with one tiny leaf.

My face beamed with joy. In that quiet moment I remembered: *flames are also purifying.*

Trouble in our lives can feel like flames of intense heat beating against our bodies, minds, and souls. Our situation stinks like the charred limbs on the trees. Confusion, like smoke, hinders our movement and impedes our thoughts.

Maybe you feel burned, like all you have left are scorched remains. Take heart. God will bring new life to you just like the burned mountain trees.

In the Bible, God manifests Himself as fire. Exodus 3:2–4 says,

> *The Angel of the Lord appeared to him in a flame of fire from the midst of a bush. So he looked, and behold, the bush was burning with fire, but the bush was not consumed. Then Moses said, "I will now turn aside and see this great sight, why the bush does not burn." So when the Lord saw that he turned aside to look, God called to him from the midst of the bush and said, "Moses, Moses!" And he said, "Here I am."*

Several years later the Lord is still showing Himself as fire, not to one man, but to a whole nation wandering in the wilderness. Exodus 13:21 tells us, *The Lord went before them by day in a pillar of cloud to lead the way, and by night in a pillar of fire to give them light.*

The Bible also tells us God's Word purifies like fire. In Jeremiah 23:29 it is written, *"Is not My word like a fire?" says the Lord, "and like a hammer that breaks the rock in pieces?"*

And Psalm 66:10 says, *For You, O God, have tested us; You have refined us as silver is refined.*

God's Word—a fire for delight, guidance, and purification.

God's ministry to us includes taking out our hearts of stone and giving us "a heart of flesh"—a pliable heart, a heart tender toward Him.

> *I will give you a new heart and put a new spirit within you; I will take the heart of stone out of your flesh and give you a heart of flesh. I Will put My Spirit within you and cause you to walk in My statutes, and you will keep My judgments and do them* (Ezekiel 36:26–27).

God is a Refiner of hearts, a Purifier of them. *He [God] will sit as a smelter and purifier of silver, and He will purify the sons of Levi and refine them like gold and silver, so that they may present to the Lord offerings in righteousness* (Malachi 3:3).

Let's think together about what a refiner's job entails to enhance our knowledge of God's method, His purpose, and the end result of His work in us.

I'm blessed to have a friend in the jewelry-making business and understands the refining process. Brad has toured several of the largest refineries and has seen what happens with his own eyes. He shared with me the basic steps of the refiner's tasks:

> First, the ore containing precious metals is **crushed** to a powder through a series of rollers, then dumped into containers of water for the metal to settle to the bottom. The water and contaminants are poured off and the remaining metal allowed to dry.

> Next, the powder is passed through magnets to remove any iron or steel. Then the powder is dissolved in a vat of acid. The dissolved metals will settle to the bottom in order of their specific gravity. Platinum, the heaviest metal, will drop to the bottom, followed by gold, silver, and copper.

> Then the metals are separated, rinsed, and dried. Each metal is **melted** separately in a crucible usually made of high-temperature ceramic. Some crucibles are made of graphite and very large ones are made of iron. All crucibles are coated with a high temperature glaze to keep the metal from sticking and/or contaminating the precious metal.

> Any remaining contaminate will float to the top and form a skin on the surface called **dross**. The dross is scraped off with a rod made of quartz, carbon, or ceramic. Molten gold radiates with the most beautiful reddish orange glow you have ever seen. The surface of the molten gold has a mirror-like surface.

Fascinating. Thanks, Brad!

Refiners work with imperfect materials and create a valuable, precious gemstone, a beautiful jewel.

Did you notice the boldface words in Brad's explanation? Crushed. Melted. Dross.

The Bible tells us we have a Refiner. God told His people: *See, I have refined you, though not as silver; I have tested you in the furnace of affliction* (Isaiah 48:10).

The heat of God's affliction melts our hard hearts. The pain and heat of fire brings impurities and unrighteousness to the forefront, where God removes them. During this time, God is also teaching us to be dependent on Him and trust Him more.

Remove the dross from the silver and a silversmith can produce a vessel (Proverbs 25:4). In the transformation and refining process, we become a vessel God can use.

Most can recall a specific time when God was refining us. For some, the spark of anguish and the blazing grief is fresh. Others might have to travel down Memory Lane—or Scary Street—to reflect on such a trial.

In what ways are you or have you felt the squeeze or pressure of the refining process?

While in the heat, what was your gut reaction? (Circle all that apply)

- I've done something wrong.
- God is mad at me.
- God has something to teach me.
- This isn't fair.
- Other ___________________________

What did you learn in the furnace of affliction?

What dross do you think God is scraping off in your life? What would you like Him to remove? What riches is He adding?

Take heart. Recall from this week's introduction the words of Isaiah 43:2: *When you walk through the fire, you shall not be burned, nor shall the flame scorch you.* The New Living Translation says, *When you walk through the fire of oppression, you will not be burned up; the flames will not consume you.*

And Jeremiah writes in Lamentations 3:22, *Through the Lord's mercies we are not consumed, because His compassions fail not.*

In the context of this verse, the people were experiencing immediate horror—the destruction of the temple and Jerusalem, the murder of thousands, and the exile of many to Babylon. Yet "the writer remembers all the evidence of God's compassion and faithfulness in the past; he refuses to give up hope now." [95]

We have a beautiful promise from God and great consolation. Isaiah 61:3 tells us:

> [I will] *provide for those who grieve in Zion—to bestow on them a crown of beauty instead of ashes, the oil of joy instead of mourning, and a garment of praise instead of a spirit of despair. They will be called oaks of righteousness, a planting of the LORD for the display of his splendor.*

Oh, the hair on my arm is standing. Shivers brought on by amazing truth.

Crown of beauty.

Oil of joy.

Garment of praise.

Righteousness.

Splendor.

All of this—spelled out in one paragraph—is what we can anticipate!

This. This is what we have to look forward to as women of God.

Then like the mirror image, God sees His reflection in the polished woman.

What specifically are you choosing to believe from God's Word today?

Day One's Sparkling Gem: I believe God is polishing me to become a vessel He can use.

Prayer: Great Refiner, I praise You, oh God! You are faithful, and You are doing an extraordinary work in my life. Your purifying fires are transforming me and making me into a vessel You can use. I will not be consumed. Thank You for staying with me. Thank You for the crown of beauty and joy! Refiner, Your work is beautiful. In Jesus's name, amen.

Perspective: Make the lyrics of "Refiner's Fire" song be your prayer today. The words are lovely and heartfelt. Here's the YouTube link: Refiner's Fire (https://www.youtube.com/watch?v=9Y8zP34AhuU)

Stay Anchored

In order to realize the worth of the anchor we need to feel the stress of the storm.
Corrie Ten Boom[96]

Before I was afflicted I went astray, but now I keep Your word. You are good, and do good; teach me Your statutes. The proud have forged a lie against me, but I will keep Your precepts with my whole heart. Their heart is [spiritually insensible], but I delight in Your law. It is good for me that I have been afflicted, that I may learn Your statutes.
Psalm 119:67–71

Pivotal Point: Our anchor holds when we grip God's Word.

At 6:40 a.m. the roar of a school bus passing by my house awakened me. Or at least I thought the noise woke me. Maybe I was awake. My husband had just passed away ten hours and forty minutes earlier, after enduring two and one-half years of painful cancer.

Why is there school today? Don't they know?

Sitting up in bed, I recognized what a strange thought that was. Everything in my world had stopped. It didn't seem right or fair that the rest of the world was moving on. Facing this reality was more of the same—the most difficult storm of my life.

Storms. Deep waters.

We've talked about their different names: trial, pain, heat, trouble, adversity, suffering, and darkness.

Regardless of the name we give them, storms can shake our foundation. We're whisked away by the surge of emotion. Everything we thought we knew suddenly becomes uncertain.

Winds of turmoil blow in fear. We think we'll snap like pine trees.

Hailstones pound our hearts and minds.

Our struggle might be a hurricane-type storm with lasting consequences, changing the landscape of our circumstances. Or perhaps, our pain is more like a torrential rainstorm keeping us inside all day.

Drowning, gasping for air.

Will I ever breathe again?

Perhaps the heaviness is similar to a snowdrift pressing against our back.

Will I be crushed under the weight of my burdens?

Recall in Psalm 69:1–2 David used "mire" as a metaphor for pain and trouble. Mire is defined as deep mud.[97]

Deep mud. Can you relate?

Mire, or trouble, could be:

- Broken relationships
- Stressful work-related situations
- Disappointments
- Financial upheaval
- Health issues
- Consequences of unwise decisions
- Infidelity
- Cancer
- Death
- Betrayal
- Job loss
- Depression

Lots of troubles.

With His disciples in a boat on the Sea of Galilee, Jesus encountered a raging storm. Although the winds tossed the boat around like a toy, Jesus slept. The disciples, gripped with fear, woke up their leader. Then with power and authority, Jesus calmed the storm (Mark 4:35–41).

Are you in the midst of a raging storm? If so, how would you describe your trouble? In what ways do you need Jesus to meet your needs?

Sweet comfort and assurance can be found in Psalm 107:28–29: *They cry out to the Lord in their trouble, and He brings them out of their distresses. He calms the storm, so that its waves are still.*

Recall Matthew 14:28–30. We mentioned this verse briefly in Week Two:

> *And Peter answered Him and said, "Lord, if it is You, command me to come to You on the water." So He said, "Come." And when Peter had come down out of the boat, he walked on the water to go to Jesus. But when he saw that the wind was boisterous, he was afraid; and beginning to sink he cried out, saying, "Lord, save me!"*

In this brief but powerful passage, Jesus extended His hand to Peter and asked him to get out of the boat and come toward Him. Peter did.

While he kept his eyes on Jesus, what was the outcome?

When Peter looked away and saw the vastness of the wind and sea—serious problems—he became afraid. What happened next?

What is the implication when we put eyes on Jesus? What is the consequence when we don't?

What problem(s) are you facing?

While sloshing through storms, the terrifying circumstances can steal our joy, scramble our focus, and create huge distractions, diverting our attention away from God. But it doesn't have to be this way.

Hebrews 12:2 tells us, *Fix[ing]our eyes on Jesus, the pioneer and perfecter of faith* (NIV).

Paul instructs: *Set your mind on things above, not on things on the earth* (Colossians 3:2).

And Isaiah 26:3 says, *You will keep him in perfect peace, whose mind is stayed on You, because he trusts in You.*

We don't have to sink in the storm. We can fix our eyes on Jesus by:

- Thinking about Him
- Believing He sees our situation
- Reading the Bible and applying its teaching to our circumstances
- Believing His words
- Talking with Him
- Trusting God to bring good from bad
- Staying humble and dependent on Him

We won't be pulled out to sea to drown. Jesus is our anchor. See for yourself. Match these verses to their reference.

This hope we have as an anchor of the soul, both sure and steadfast.	Psalm 62:5
My beloved brethren, be steadfast, immovable, always abounding in the work of the Lord, knowing that your labor is not in vain in the Lord.	Hebrews 6:19

| *My soul, wait in silence for God alone, for my hope is from Him.* | 1 Corinthians 15:58 |

Courageous is Her Name

Meet a woman who lived through frightening circumstances and continuous adversity but believed God was her hope.

Rahab is identified as a promiscuous woman. She lived in Jericho, the gateway city to Canaan. Her home, situated on the wall surrounding Jericho, was used as a place to entertain men. While engaged with the locals and tourists alike, Rahab heard many stories.

One tale impacted her. Someone told her about how the God of the Israelites had dried up the Red Sea so they could escape from their Egyptian slave masters.

Now that's good gossip.

Later, Joshua, the appointed leader of the Israelites, sent two spies into Jericho to check out the city. By God's divine intervention, they found safety in Rahab's house.

Maybe you know this story. Maybe not.

Let's refresh our memory and visualize the events of this astonishing story. Read Joshua 2:1–21.

Where did Rahab hide the spies? (v. 6)

Why did she decide to rescue them? (vv. 8–10)

Where did her hope come from? (v.11)

What did she ask for as payment for hiding them? (vv. 12–13)

How did the spies respond to her request? (v. 14)

What did Rahab use to lower them down the city wall? (v. 15)

What warning did she give them? (v.16)

What did Rahab put in the window upon their return? (v.18)

What evidence was there to prove she would honor their request and their God? (v. 21)

Rahab's actions, words, warnings, and responses give us insight into her character. Rahab courageously anchored herself to God, which enabled her to carry out God's plan.

And her house?

Her residence was transformed from a place of scandalous behavior to a lighthouse on a hill.

On the seventh day, Israel marches into battle. Rahab heard the blast of the rams' horns, and the thunder of the crumbling city walls. Can you imagine the mayhem outside her window? What do you think was going through her mind?

Fast-forward to Joshua Chapter Six. The city had been destroyed, its people were defeated. The battle was over.

What was next? A mission trip!

Right. Rahab's first mission trip was to her family, where she led them to believe in the God of Abraham. Her entire household was saved—rescued from the storm.

We too have hope of an awe-inspiring transformation. Second Corinthians 3:18 tells us, *But we all, with unveiled face, beholding as in a mirror the glory of the Lord, are being transformed into the same image from glory to glory, just as by the Spirit of the Lord.*

And Psalm 71:20 tells us, *Though You have made me see troubles, many and bitter, You will restore my life again; from the depths of the earth you will again bring me up* (NIV).

During adversity, we can ask ourselves two questions:

1. What does God want me to learn?
2. What does God want to do through me?

John 8:12 tells us to follow Jesus: *The one who follows me will not walk in darkness.*

Hang onto Jesus, your Anchor. Then, like Rahab, you'll be a beacon in the dark drawing others to the Light.

What specifically are you choosing to believe from God's Word today?

Day Two's Sparkling Gem: I believe Jesus is my anchor, and I won't drown in this storm.

Prayer: Savior, my Anchor, oh how I need You! Sometimes I feel I'm in over my head. But I know You are holding me. You are my hope and I trust fully in You. Remind me each day how You are transforming me into the image of Christ and becoming a vessel You can use. Open my eyes to see what You want me to see. In Jesus's name I pray, Amen.

Perspective: As instructed, Rahab used a red cord to show her faithfulness. Show your faithfulness and tie a red ribbon around something (like a flowerpot) to remind you to keep your eyes fixed on God.

Week Four, Day 3

Genuine Joy

Hope itself is like a star—not to be seen in the sunshine of prosperity, and only to be discovered in the night of adversity.
Charles Spurgeon[98]

Therefore you now have sorrow; but I will see you again and your heart will rejoice, and your joy no one will take from you. And in that day you will ask Me nothing. Most assuredly, I say to you, whatever you ask the Father in My name He will give you. Until now you have asked nothing in My name. Ask, and you will receive, that your joy may be full.
John 16:22–24

Pivotal Point: Our joy emerges when we focus on God's character and His promises.

Many people are searching for joy.

When I typed "how to find joy" into my internet search engine, hundreds of articles popped up. One secular article listed twenty-five ways to have joy. God's name and the Bible were not mentioned. The ideas listed were not harmful or immoral. In fact, most felt familiar, like I had read them before. And I had … in the Bible.

That irritates me. Taking ownership of an idea that was God's idea first.

For example, one recommendation credited Oprah, who said, "Be grateful." However, she didn't say to whom or to what we should direct our gratitude. She didn't say be grateful to God.

Another suggestion was encourage your friends by writing a card or sending a text.

Ugh.

God's idea. I'll show you. *Encourage one another and build one another up, just as you also are doing* (1 Thessalonians 5:11 NASB).

One might as well keep searching the internet for suggestions because here's the thing: living separate from the Creator of joy, lasting joy is not obtainable.

Recall James 1:2: *My brethren, count it all joy when you fall into various trials.*

In this context the word *count* suggests we tally the reasons for joy. For most of us, joy in suffering goes against our human tendencies and may not feel achievable.

King David is honored in Scripture because of his habitual praise and thanksgiving to God throughout the psalms. Despite his circumstances, his roller-coaster emotions, his sin, his perceptions, his rants, and doubts, he came back with praise to God. David knew God was worthy of thanksgiving and would always triumph. When David offered praise, he focused on God, not himself. His praise brought glory to God and demonstrated faithful obedience.

Although he may not have realized it, his praise protected and grounded him—for praise is the bridge to joy.

Joy is a little word, but when a woman is joyful, big changes occur.

Take a look at synonyms for joy: bubbly, lighthearted, good-humored.

Joy doesn't necessarily mean feeling happy. Rather, joy is clinging to God's truth and finding contentment in Him despite the circumstances. As a result, a joyful person exudes an optimistic, hopeful attitude. People from all cultures and religions notice this kind of joyful mindset.

Joy comes from believing what God says and applying His truths moment by moment.

Have you ever experienced a hard time, yet you were full of joy? If so, write about it. If not, what kept you from having joy?

Being joyful doesn't mean we put on an act. Neither does joy indicate our lives are perfect. Joy results when we look to God and study His attributes.

Read Psalm 34:5 and fill in the missing word:

Those who look to Him are ____.

Most translations use the same word—*radiant*. But the KJV uses lightened. How would you describe a radiant person? Would joyful be part of your description? Why or why not?

During the most painful time of my life, I was uncertain about *how* God would keep His promises. But I had assurance *He would*. He had proved Himself faithful in the past. and I trusted Him in the present. His faithfulness filled me with joy, not my situation.

I clung to many verses in the Bible. One in particular was 2 Corinthians 4:7–9 which says:

> *But we have this treasure in earthen vessels, that the excellence of the power may be of God and not of us. We are hard-pressed on every side, yet not crushed; we are perplexed, but not in despair; persecuted, but not forsaken; struck down, but not destroyed.*

I asked myself, "Do you believe this verse?"

Scrutinizing the words, I applied them to my personal trial. Here is what mine looked like:

I am hard-pressed:

I feel pressure to know what to say, to be happy enough, or sad enough, or live up to other people's expectations of me.

But not crushed:

With the power of God, I can let go of these demands.

I am perplexed:

I have questions, just as the disciples did after Jesus told them He was leaving.

But not is despair:

Talking to God and believing Him helps me not dwell on the same thoughts that lead to despair. God knows what I do not know.

I am persecuted:

I am in a hard place, struggling through the longest trial I've faced.

But not forsaken:

God is with me. He will never abandon me.

I am struck down:

Alone. Dealing with the unknown. Unsure.

But not destroyed:

God lifts me up to persevere. He is making a way for me.

The answers became my tally of joy.

Your turn. Write your answers. Speak aloud in confidence the reason you won't be destroyed. You're planting a seed in which joy can grow.

I am hard-pressed with

____

____

____

____

But not crushed because

____

____

____

____

I am perplexed about

____

____

____

But not in despair because

____

____

____

____

I am persecuted

____

____

____

____

But not forsaken because

____

____

____

____

I am struck down with

____

____

____

____

But not destroyed because

____

____

____

____

During my suffering, I was simultaneously sad and joyful. Sad my husband had passed away, but joyful knowing God was in control. A miraculous oxymoron!

God will do the same for you.

Colossians 1:13–14 tells us:

> _He has delivered us from the power of darkness and conveyed us into the kingdom of the Son of His love, in whom we have redemption through His blood, the forgiveness of sins._

Darkness enslaves. We can live in joy under the authority of the Son.

At the time of this writing, one of the most meaningful, life-preserving verses for me is one Paul, the man who was beaten and imprisoned, wrote as a concluding prayer of exhortation. He said in Romans 15:13, *Now may the God of hope fill you with all joy and peace in believing, that you may abound in hope by the power of the Holy Spirit.*

Put a box around each of these phrases and words: *God of hope, all joy, and peace, believing, abound.*

A quick look in the dictionary defines abound as "large numbers or in great quantity." [99]

When we believe, God lavishes hope in salvation and in our expectations, with joy and peace.

Every morning and throughout the day, I speak this verse back to God as my prayer:

> *God, You are my hope. You said You would give me joy. So here I am... pour it on me. And You said I can have peace in this difficult time. Okay, give me peace. You said I would abound in hope—give me tons of hope, please! Yes, God, I believe!*

Hope, peace, and joy. Totally obtainable because we ask of God.

No shock.

No surprise.

When we focus on Him, Psalm 16:11 tells us, *You will show me the path of life; in Your presence is fullness of joy.*

Joy doesn't have to be a future destination. Joy can accompany us on our journeys every day when our focus shifts from our circumstances to God's greatness.

Believe. Jeremiah 31:25 tells us, *I have satiated [satisfied] the weary soul, and I have replenished every sorrowful soul.*

In the New Living Translation this verse reads, *I have given rest to the weary and joy to the sorrowing.*

We started this lesson with the world's prescription for finding joy. I've created twenty-five Bible-based ways for experiencing genuine, sustainable joy at the end of this chapter. I've applied all of them at one time or another.

Remember, our storms won't last forever. John 12:46 tells us, *I have come as a light into the world, that whoever believes in Me should not abide in darkness.*

What specifically are you choosing to believe from God's Word today?

Day Three's Sparkling Gem: I believe I can simultaneously experience trials with a radiant countenance and joyful attitude.

Prayer: Dear God of Hope, without You there'd be no purpose for living or any reason to get out of bed in the morning or even walk out the door. You, God, are my everything. You are the beautiful Light shining through me. You are my strength and the reason I am joyful today. Continue to fill me with joy. In Jesus's name, amen.

Perspective: Start a gratitude journal. Each day write ten things you're grateful for. Then tell God thank you. Be grateful also for what didn't happen—those people and events God protected you from.

1. Read your Bible and *believe* what it says. Apply its words to your life moment by moment. During a sad time in my life Romans 15:13 was a daily hope—like medicine: *Now may the God of hope fill you with all joy and peace in believing, that you may abound in hope by the power of the Holy Spirit.* After my husband passed away, there were many mornings that before getting out of bed I'd lay quietly while tears trickled down my face. Soon, though, I'd make my way to the kitchen. This is the place I learned to hold my hands toward heaven as if waiting to receive. I'd reiterate this verse to God. He faithfully provided, and I was able to go about my work with joy. I would repeat this habit every day.

2. Stay active physically. Walking produces endorphins that are good for you.

3. Be productive. Use your skills, talents, and abilities.

4. Pray. Tell God the truth about what's troubling you. One morning I was cleaning out my husband's dresser. Two hours passed and I realized I was becoming gloomy. I prayed and asked God to renew my spirit. He spoke to my heart and told me to take a break and not work so long at this task. So I stopped and invited a friend to lunch. My entire mindset changed! Remember 2 Corinthians 4:16: *We do not lose heart. Even though our outward man is perishing, yet the inward man is being renewed day by day.*

5. Reflect on beautiful memories, beautiful things, and beautiful people.

6. Remember God's faithfulness to you in the past. Rest in His presence and ponder the great things He's done. Tell Him again how you're grateful. Psalm 103:2 says, *Bless the Lord, O my soul, and forget not all His benefits.*

7. Life is short and unpredictable. Make the most of every opportunity. The Bible tells us in Ephesians to *Walk circumspectly, not as fools but as wise, redeeming the time, because the days are evil* (5:15–16).

8.   Stuff is temporary. Share what you have now, because one day it's all going away.

9.   Sing along to worship songs and visualize the words. Paint or color the lyrics. Psalm 90:14 says, *Sing for joy and be glad* (NASB). Isn't it cool that God knows when we sing praises to Him, we experience joy?

10.   Believe. You are on this earth for a purpose. Get on it. Psalm 16:11 says, *You will show me the path of life; in Your presence is fullness of joy; at Your right hand are pleasures forevermore.*

11.   Seek godly counsel if necessary to help you devise a plan and make goals.

12.   Realize your need for rest. Some things can wait. Find your balance.

13.   Talk about God. The biography found in Psalm 103 is a good place to start. Share how God has been these things to you.

14.   Believe it's okay to cry. God created tears. Psalm 56:8 says, [God] *Put my tears into Your bottle.* Archaeologists have discovered small "tear bottles" which mourners used to collect their tears, then bury them at a gravesite. With this bottle was a note that explained their deep sorrow. Tears in a bottle is a remembrance. God's Word tells us that He chronicles our tears.

15.   Surround yourself with friends who offer you support, love, accountability, and are willing to cry and laugh with you, help you rest, and have fun.

16.   Appreciate every day as a new beginning. Recall Lamentations 3:22–23: *Through the Lord's mercies we are not consumed, because His compassions fail not. They are new every morning; great is Your faithfulness.*

17.   Understand it's okay to not be okay. It's also okay to be okay. You're not strange in this regard.

18.   Make it your goal to tell God specific things you're thankful for each and every day.

19.   Tell others the impact they've had on your life. Write a card or send a text.

20.   Volunteer at a church, shelter, school, orphanage, retirement center, or any other worthwhile organization.

21.   Write favorite Bible verses on sticky notes and place them in conspicuous places like on your mirror, coffee pot, refrigerator, or car dashboard. I have porcelain place cards placed around my house. For example, Isaiah 50:4 is written on a place card at my coffee pot: *Morning by morning he wakens me and opens my understanding to his will* (NLT). Another one is in my windowsill and reminds me that whatever happens today, God has already made a plan to work it out: *It shall come to pass that before they call, I will answer; and while they are still speaking, I will hear* (Isaiah 65:24).

22.   Realize your trial will end and that God will bring good from it. We have this promise in Romans 8:28: *And we know that all things work together for good to those who love God, to those who are the called according to His purpose.*

23.   Speak the name of Jesus aloud. Or Yahweh. Or any other name for God. After my husband passed but four days before his service, I had a scheduled routine yearly doctor's appointment. When I arrived, the nurse asked me the general questions. I shared with her the challenges of the past year and that my husband had just passed away. After she took my blood pressure, she remarked that it was high. I'd never had high blood pressure before. She left the room, and I sat in silence. Then I took several deep breaths—breathing in and out *Yawah*. When the nurse returned, I asked her to retake my blood pressure. With a curious look she said, "Wow, it's normal now."

24.   Purchase a Bible study about joy and work through it with a group.

25.   Read Bible-based books about joy. There are many!

Biography Of God Based on Psalm 103

What is God like? He is:

Compassionate

Gracious

Slow to anger

Merciful

Understanding

Aware

Everlasting

Established

Sovereign

What does God do? He:

Pardons

Heals

Redeems

Shows love

Shows kindness

Satisfies

Gives good things

Does righteous deeds

Judges right

Shows the way

Acts on my behalf

Forgives

Bless the Lord, Oh my soul!

Week Four, Day 4

You're Grounded

Let us not be surprised when we have to face difficulties. When the wind blows hard on a tree, the roots stretch and grow the stronger. Let it be so with us. Let us not be weaklings, yielding to every wind that blows, but strong in spirit to resist.
Amy Carmichael[100]

Blessed is the man who trusts in the Lord, and whose hope is the Lord. For he shall be like a tree planted by the waters, which spreads out its roots by the river, and will not fear when heat comes; but its leaf will be green, and will not be anxious in the year of drought, nor will cease from yielding fruit.
Jeremiah 17:7–8

Pivotal Point: Our hope stays grounded when rooted in Christ.

Once when I was picking tomatoes from the vine, I reached for what appeared to be a gorgeous plump tomato screaming to be eaten on a mayonnaise sandwich. But when I got closer, I discovered it was rotten. The tomato had become separated from the vine and was squashed against the ground.

That's disappointing.

You know what else can be disappointing? A trial. Like a weed that spouts up in our well-manicured garden.

Confusion and disillusionment muddies the water. Sadness fills our heart.

We might feel disconnected from God, a bit like that rotten tomato, squashed between unmet expectations and what we think is fair.

Unable to see things from His perspective.

Mushy.

You know, not firm.

When darkness hovers it can be difficult to produce good fruit—unless we're connected to the vine. Jesus tells us, *"I am the true vine, and My Father is the vinedresser"* (John 15:1).

Aversity is an opportunity for God to prune our character if we'll allow Him. The process is often painful but yields good fruit.

Let's continue reading John 15:2–5.

> *Every branch in Me that does not bear fruit He takes away; and every branch that bears fruit He prunes, that it may bear more fruit. You are already clean because of the word which I have spoken to you. Abide in Me, and I in you. As the branch cannot bear fruit of itself, unless it abides in the vine, neither can you, unless you abide in Me. "I am the vine, you are the branches. He who abides in Me, and I in him, bears much fruit; for without Me you can do nothing.*

What does the vinedresser's pruning accomplish?

What do you think it means to *abide* with Jesus?

During the refining process, God cuts away sinful habits or selfish attitudes, and removes what is hurtful. His pruning enables new growth, including equipping us for a specific task, event, or relationship.

Have you felt the painful effects of God's pruning tools recently? What do you believe God is cutting from you or preparing in you?

When we connect to the Vine our roots grow deep and produce the fruit of peace and joy, even in pain.

How Do We Get Grounded?

I was listening to an actor being interviewed on one of the morning news shows several years ago. He was asked how he prepared for a movie role. He answered, "You start to feel more like the character and think like he would, the more you spend time with him."

I loved his answer.

While the actor referred to time spent with the person he was portraying, the implication for Christ-followers is the same: We need to spend time with God, reading the Bible. As we discover God's character, our faith will grow because *faith comes by hearing, and hearing by the word of God* (Romans 10:17). The more time we spend with God, the more fruit we produce.

More life-giving truth is found in Psalm 1.

> *Blessed is the man who walks not in the counsel of the ungodly, nor stands in the path of sinners, nor sits in the seat of the scornful; but his delight is in the law of the Lord, and in His law he meditates day and night. He shall be like a tree planted by the rivers of water, that brings forth its fruit in its season, whose leaf also shall not wither; and whatever he does shall prosper. The ungodly are not so, but are like the chaff which the wind drives away. Therefore the ungodly shall not stand in the judgment, nor sinners in the congregation of the righteous. For the Lord knows the way of the righteous, but the way of the ungodly shall perish.*

What does the Psalm One Woman delight in?

How often does she spend time in God's word?

To what is she compared?

What does this woman's deep roots provide?

A refined woman is like this tree whose roots are firmly established and able to stretch to the river to receive strength and nourishment from living waters. She entwines her roots around the Bible and ponders God's sustaining words. Then, when the storms blow in, she won't be whisked away, for her strong root system keeps her grounded. When the season of drought descends on her, neither will she wither. When it's time to prune her limbs, she may experience discomfort, but this trimming enables her to produce beautiful, sweet-smelling fruit of the Spirit.

As Christ-followers, God meets us in our dry places, providing rest and refreshment.

Isaiah 58:11 tells us, *The Lord will guide you continually, and satisfy your soul in drought, and strengthen your bones; you shall be like a watered garden, and like a spring of water, whose waters do not fail.*

What is the evidence that you are well-watered, connected, and grounded?

Ephesians 3:16–18 tells us, *Being rooted and established in love, may have power, together with all the Lord's holy people, to grasp how wide and long and high and deep is the love of Christ* (NIV).

How does your love for God, and your recognition of His love for you, enable you to love others?

Take a moment to evaluate your root system. On a scale from 1-10 with 10 being the strongest, how grounded are your roots?

| 1 | 2 | 3 | 4 | 5 | 6 | 7 | 8 | 9 | 10 |

Colossians 2:6–7 tells us:

> *As you therefore have received Christ Jesus the Lord, so walk in Him, rooted and built up in Him and established in the faith, as you have been taught, abounding in it with thanksgiving.*

Chill bumps are running up my arm.

That's what happens when something so divinely significant or poignant grabs my attention. A footnote accompanying this verse says: "When we continue to walk with Christ, we are by God's power, rooted in Him like a strong tree and built up in Him like a beautiful building."[101]

Rooted. Standing. Strong.

A pillar built up in Him like a beautiful building who:

- Bears the fruit of joy, peace, and patience in trials
- Believes trials are temporary
- Asks "What does God want me to learn from this?"
- Doesn't need to fake a positive outlook
- Shows gratitude to God despite the difficult season
- Believes the life-giving counsel discovered in God's Word
- Knows her true identity and worth
- Remains unshakable

First Corinthians 15:58 says, *Therefore, my dear brothers and sisters, stand firm. Let nothing move you. Always give yourselves fully to the work of the Lord, because you know that your labor in the Lord is not in vain* (NIV).

Are your roots getting stronger? How so? What outcomes would you like to see?

The trials we face have been sifted through the hand of God and have purpose. Stay connected and grounded. Then, regardless of the circumstances we'll be able to *cast off the works of darkness, and ... put on the armor of light* (Romans 13:12).

What specifically are you choosing to believe from God's Word today?

Day Four's Sparkling Gem: I believe when I'm grounded in Jesus, my roots will sustain me in adversity, and He will bring me through trials victoriously.

Prayer: Dear Father, my Vinedresser, I submit. Prune everything rotten in me. Refresh my spirit in drought. Help me to grow strong roots in You. I am reminded of Psalm 9:9, which says, "You, Lord, are my refuge, a stronghold in my time of trouble." I thirst for everything good and righteous. I thirst for You alone. Water me today. I love You. In Jesus's name, amen.

Perspective: Purchase a house plant that needs to be watered regularly. A fern is an excellent choice. They need lots of water. The task of watering will remind you to water yourself with God's Word.

Week Four, Day 5

Remaining Faithful

Remember Whose you are and Whom you serve. Provoke yourself by recollection, and your affection for God will increase tenfold; your imagination will not be starved any longer, but will be quick and enthusiastic, and your hope will be inexpressibly bright.
Oswald Chambers[102]

Trust in the Lord, and do good; dwell in the land, and feed on His faithfulness. Delight yourself also in the Lord, and He shall give you the desires of your heart. Commit your way to the Lord, trust also in Him, and He shall bring it to pass.
Psalm 37:3–5

Pivotal Point: Our faith remains firm as God strengthens our hearts.

"God, you've always been faithful to me," I said.

Sitting on the bench in my yard, the breeze cooled my skin as orange and yellow leaves floated to the ground. Autumn usually reminds me of God's faithfulness. But that day, I wasn't only recalling the past. I was also imploring God to stay faithful as my husband and I walked through the horrible storm of his cancer diagnosis and treatments.

"I've trusted You as my Savior since when I was only nine years old. And since then, You've been faithful."

Through tears I continued, "I believe You'll be faithful now."

I sat motionless and quiet. Recalling God's devotion was medicine to my soul. And as I spoke the words aloud, I felt peace.

After what seemed to be only a minute, however, I sensed a nudge. A gentle impression bubbled inside me, and God whispered to my heart.

I will. But will you remain faithful to me?

In the midst of a dark season came a convicting, life-changing, moment.

I think I'm faithful.

What do you think it means to be faithful to God?

Recall Galatians 5:22: *But the fruit of the Spirit is ... faithfulness.*

When we're trudging through a dark period, our emotions can swing unexpectedly from one end of the pendulum to the other. We can, however, remain faithful to God when we keep in step with the Spirit.

Let's walk together and examine five ways to stay faithful.

Remain Faithful to God By Giving Him Your Devotion

James, the half-brother of Jesus, makes a strong accusation. Read James 4:4. With what does he charge them?

The unbelievers? No. Unbelievers can't betray someone to whom they don't belong.

James is writing to Christ-followers.

In this passage, James confronted his Christian brothers and sisters with their unfaithful behavior and indifference to God.

James uses the word *adulteress*.

Wow, strong word.

Yet, correct. The Greek word for adulteress is *moichalis*.

Moichalis indicates that God's intimate alliance with the people of Israel was like a marriage. When they reverted into idolatry, God accused them of committing adultery or playing the harlot.[103]

God expresses His heart in Ezekiel 6:9: *I was crushed by their adulterous heart which has departed from Me, and by their eyes which play the harlot after their idols.*

Are you surprised by His emotion? Why or why not?

God doesn't reveal His emotion in Jeremiah 3:19, but He states what He hoped His people would do: *I thought you would call me Father, and not turn away from following me* (NIV).

What does God want us to call Him?

In what way does this effect how often we should run to the Father?

James charged the Christ-followers with this same kind of spiritual adultery—being unfaithful to God and placing faith in someone or something else, creating an idol.

Yep, an idol.

I like Charles F. Stanley's definition: "An idol is anything you value more—either by your attitude or actions—than God."[104]

Conviction. Or Confrontation with ourselves.

Is there anything in your life you value more than God? Does the time you spend with God show He's your first priority? Or does something else get most of your attention?

First Kings 8:61 tells us, *Let your heart therefore be loyal to the Lord our God, to walk in His statutes and keep His commandments, as at this day.*

We can ask our Father to show us the idols in our life. He will strengthen us so we can remove it.

Remain Faithful to God By Listening to Him

Maybe you've had this thought before. Or said it to your children: "Oh, my people need to listen to me." I sure have.

But these are the words of God found in Psalm 81:13: *Oh, that **My** people would listen to **Me*** (emphasis mine).

Jesus speaks too. John 10:3–4 tells us:

> *To him the doorkeeper opens, and the sheep hear his voice; and he calls his own sheep by name and leads them out. And when he brings out his own sheep, he goes before them; and the sheep follow him, for they know his voice.*

Our Shepherd clearly articulates His people follow Him because they hear His whisper, His nudging, His impression.

God wouldn't tell us to listen if He didn't have something to say.

The Bible is the primary place we hear God's voice. What other places and ways does God speak?

How does God speak to you in nature?

What does every sunrise say?

What does each predictable low and high tide speak?

What does God say through the chirping birds?

What does the mountain say of God's power?

If we look and listen, we can hear God. Sometimes, though, our hearing is hindered.

Busyness, our cultures propaganda, and the noise we create or surround ourselves with, may drown out the gentle voice of God.

Read John 16:13. With what does the Holy Spirit help us?

How can you be intentional about looking and listening for God's voice?

Psalm 5:3 tells us, *My voice You shall hear in the morning, O LORD; in the morning I will direct it to You, and I will look up.*

And Jeremiah 22:29 says: *O earth, earth, earth, hear the word of the LORD!*

Blessed are those who hear the word of God and keep it! (Luke 11:28)

Stay Faithful to God by Trusting Him

One day while having lunch with a dear friend, I poured out my broken heart.

"I trust God, but I'm worried about the future," I sobbed. "This cancer journey has been long and hard!"

I texted my fears to my husband, who was at work.

I was humbled and surprised, even convicted, at his response.

"Don't cry," he said. "Everything's going to work out the way God wants it to."

Didn't I trust God?

In my darkness a light emerged.

Am I willing to let God have His way regardless of the outcome? Do I trust Him?

Have you ever had to choose between your way and God's way? If so, what was the result?

God tells us to give Him our burdens (1 Peter 5:7) and the desires of our heart (Psalm 20:4).

I did both. But a deeper truth surfaced.

Your desires, God, must trump mine.

My worry disabled my faith and immobilized my ability to trust God.

What do you need to trust God with?

We either trust God or we don't. There isn't an in-between.

Proverbs 3:5–6 tells us:

> Trust in the LORD with all your heart, and lean not on your own understanding; in all your ways acknowledge Him, and He shall direct your paths.

Remain Faithful to God by Waiting on His Timing

Waiting may be the most difficult when we're waiting for a trial to end.

If we knew the end result was going to be good, we might stop praying, which would deprive us of deep conversations with God.

Conversely, if we knew the end result would be bad, we might feel defeated and hopeless or angry at God.

We wait because certain things need to be in place before other things happen. Specific beliefs and attitudes have to be nurtured and lessons must be learned.

Waiting is like holding a plank. Our whole body is quivering, yet we're becoming stronger.

Are you waiting? If so, what is the most difficult part?

Romans 12:12 tells us, *Rejoicing in hope, patient in tribulation, continuing steadfastly in prayer.*

And Isaiah 40:31 says, *But those who wait on the LORD shall renew their strength; they shall mount up with wings like eagles, they shall run and not be weary, they shall walk and not faint.*

Resist rushing ahead of God if you think He's lingering or not listening. He's doing a perfect work and He *is* listening. Don't stop praying … we have so much hope!

Remain Faithful to God by Remembering

Recall part of the lesson's opening quote from Oswald Chambers: "Provoke yourself by recollection, and your affection for God will increase tenfold."

I wish I had said that.

When I reflect on God's goodness in the past, I grow to love and trust Him more. I believe His promises because I've seen how He's kept them.

Read Psalm 111:2. What does this verse tell us to do?

Most versions say "study" or" ponder."

The footnote in my New King James Version says, "to understand and make connections."[105]

Recall—not in shame or guilt, but to grasp the impact of God's intervention.

What situation has God rescued you from? What attitude has He freed you from?

Looking back on God's faithfulness becomes your hope for the future. Then Psalm145:4 tells us to *declare Your mighty acts.* This becomes our testimony that draws others to Him.

God is working in our dark season—polishing, refining, strengthening, preparing, and teaching.

Remember, Jesus said, *"I have come as a light into the world, that whoever believes in Me should not abide in darkness."*

Oh, girl, this is good news. God's Spirit will pierce the darkness.

Despite our trials, we'll stay faithful and shine!

We're ready to stand as a pillar in our home and community. Let's move on to Week Five and discuss this further.

What specifically are you choosing to believe from God's Word today?

Day Five's Sparkling Gem: I believe choosing to walk in the Spirit enables me to be faithful.

Prayer: Faithful Father, thank You for your faithfulness to me over my entire life. You have proved Yourself faithful again and again. You have never lied, nor have You ever failed me. Father God, I ask You to keep me faithful. Help me to trust You better. Open my eyes to see more of Your character. Empower me to surrender my selfish desires. I want Your will. I want Your way. I love You and no other. In Jesus's name, amen.

Perspective: One of my favorite songs to sing (or sign) is "The Goodness of God." Within the lyrics are the words: "All my life you have been faithful." This is true of my life and reminds me to be faithful back to God. You can listen to the song here: The Goodness of God (https://www.youtube.com/watch?v=PvkpeJ-Xd1U)

<u>**Introduction: Week Five—She's a Pillar and Cornerstone**</u>

Participants Guide

Priscilla means, *venerable*: "commanding respect because of great
_________________ or impressive _______________________; worthy of
____________________.

Working together made Priscilla and Aquilla both stand out as
____
____.

A cornerstone joins ____.

The cornerstone is
____.

A woman has the potential and capacity to be _______________________ a
cornerstone.

God empowers and enables all women—
s____________________________________,

m____________________________________,

w___________________________, or

d_______________________________, to function as pillars.

View Introduction:
Week Five Video on YouTube:

Our journey through this study has helped us either uncover or rediscover God's perspective, design, and purpose for women. Do you believe Him?

I love to linger here, in these eleven words used to describe God's vision for women:

That our daughters may be as pillars, sculptured in palace style.

Oh, I feel energized! I want to shout this truth from the rooftops and carry the light into the dark streets for all daughters, mothers, sisters, and friends to see. You, too? Who are you most eager to tell?

The King James Version uses the word *corner stone* (as two words) whereas the New King James Version uses *pillars*.

Back in Week Three's Introduction, I quoted Matthew Henry's comments about pillars:

> By daughters, families are united and connected, to their mutual strength, as the parts of a building are by the corner stones ... we see our daughters well-established and stayed with wisdom and discretion, as corner stones are fastened in the building ... we see them purified and consecrated to God as living temples.[106]

Henry's compelling words deepen our understanding. When women are dependent on God's multi-faceted wisdom, they become essential building materials. So, let's start building and allow ourselves to become crucial building materials.

We launched our study with Esther, the orphan who was divinely adopted into her uncle's loving Jewish family. We cracked the door open enough to see the light of

God's purpose unfolding. The light grew brighter when the young woman became queen of the Persian empire. Further exploration enabled us to grasp how courageous, beautiful, and wise she was—a refined daughter of God and a pillar in her community.

As we are nearing the end of our study, I want to introduce you to a New Testament woman who was a pillar of her community also.

I actually don't know a lot about her.

I'm unaware of her hair color, height, weight, or any physical features. I'm unfamiliar with her upbringing, hobbies, or if she ever had a spa treatment. Yet I admire her. I desire to be like her.

Meet Priscilla.

Her name means, *venerable*: "commanding respect because of great age or impressive dignity; worthy of reverence."[107]

Unlike Esther, Priscilla's story doesn't unfold in an entire book of the Bible. We do, however, gain insight about her from information sprinkled throughout the New Testament.

In Acts 18, we discover Priscilla was married to Aquila (vv.1–2). We also learn Priscilla and her husband spent time with Paul and accompanied him on mission journeys (v.18). Additionally, Priscilla and her husband were educated and wise, with a keen understanding of the Scriptures. They helped other Jewish-Christian missionaries better understand the gospel. (v.26).

Romans 16:3–4 provides more information on how this power-couple spent their days and what they were willing to do for their friend Paul:

> *Greet Priscilla and Aquila, my fellow workers in Christ Jesus, who risked their own necks for my life.*

Risked their own necks?

We may not fully grasp the details of this risky situation, but based on my experiences with friendships, only my most loyal friends would jeopardize their reputation for me. And although they love me, they wouldn't put their life in danger for me. We can conclude then, that Priscilla was a loyal friend and a courageous fighter for Jesus Christ. She was a teacher and leader, nurturing early Christians during a time of great opposition. She and Aquila established one of the first churches in their home (1 Corinthians 16:19).

Clearly, being a teacher, leader, nurturer, and builder of the early church makes Priscilla a pillar in the community!

Aquila and Priscilla worked as tentmakers (Acts 18:3). The tents were sewn together with strong cloth made from goat hair. Scripture tells us Paul stayed with them for over a year and worked alongside them in their tent-making trade. Since Priscilla worked with her hands stitching tents, it's possible she made other items—maybe clothing or household goods.

What's intriguing is the sentence structure in Romans 16:3. Paul greets the couple, naming Priscilla first. Putting the woman's name ahead of her husband's was unusual during this time period. This small but important detail suggests Priscilla's ministry stood out.

How do you think Priscilla overcame the inequality between men and women during this time period? I mean, it must have been a challenge to work with men 2,000 years ago.

Yet, we can infer that there was respect between Aquilla and Priscilla.

Priscilla is a role model. Her service along men can help women today.

Working together made Priscilla and Aquilla both stand out as pillars of their community.

You may be CEO of a company with authority over hundreds of people (much like Esther). Or you could be a Sunday school teacher in your small community church (much like Priscilla). Either way, you're an essential part to building a godly community, which starts with seeking after God.

To aid our understanding of this pillar-role, look at the following words:

foundation	basis	keystone	mainspring
mainstay	importance	functional	worth
necessary	centerpiece	core	heart
center	focus	crux	backbone
anchor	prominence	significance	influence

These words define "biblical womanhood."

And each word is similar to *cornerstone.*

Cornerstone may not be in our everyday vocabulary. We might choose to use one of the words in the previous list.

You may have a good idea of its meaning. But for general knowledge and clarity, *cornerstone* is defined this way: "A stone that forms the base of a corner of a building, joining two walls; an important quality or feature on which a particular thing depends or is based."[108]

The New Testament describes Jesus as the most important foundational stone:

> *Having been built on the foundation of the apostles and prophets, Jesus Christ Himself being the chief cornerstone* (Ephesians 2:20).
>
> *No one can lay a foundation other than that which is laid, which is Jesus Christ* (1 Corinthians 3:11).

Additionally, cornerstone is another of the messianic names of Jesus (*Yeshua*). The Hebrew word *pinna* is used in Isaiah 28:16, prophesying the Messiah will be a foundation stone in a building.[109]

To be very clear: neither women nor men, are *the* cornerstone. Jesus is the one and only Cornerstone.

According to Psalm 144:12, a woman has the potential and capacity to be *like* a cornerstone when she:

- believes God is the Builder
- uplifts her family
- applies godly wisdom to construct foundations and create bonds

- acts as a bridge to connect people
- exhibits righteous behavior
- believes in justice

What an honor to have this important position in the eyes of God.

God empowers and enables all women—single, married, widowed, or divorced—to function as pillars.

With such an important role we can conclude godly women are:

- influential
- respectable
- capable
- skilled
- qualified
- worthy
- valuable
- accomplished
- competent
- strong
- dignified
- life-giving

If you don't believe that you are these things, you're listening to the wrong voice. Write these words on separate sticky notes and place them all around your house!

This week's lessons cover building the home, community, and ultimately the nation ... because so goes the family, so goes the nation.

Now ... relax. Put down the heaviness of responsibility you envisioned descending on your shoulders. Remember, you're not the one building. The Master Builder builds *through you*. God teaches us how to build and what tools to use for indestructible foundations and unbreakable walls.

The apostle Paul writes in Colossians 1:29, *To this end I also labor, striving according to His working which works in me mightily.* God mightily works *through us.* The only question is, will we let Him?

During our fifth week, we'll talk about:

Day 1: Build the House

Day 2: Broken Walls: Don't Lose Hope

Day 3: Standing in the Gap

Day 4: Front-Door Protection and Roof-Top Prayers

Day 5: Leave the Light On

As we continue, ask God to help you believe what He says about you. Call on Him to give you strength and confidence in your role as a pillar. Ask God to give you understanding, knowledge, and wisdom to apply this cornerstone concept to your unique family, community, and situation. God loves you and the people you love. He has a plan.

Week Five, Day 1

Build the House

Therefore thus says the Lord God: "Behold, I lay in Zion a stone for a foundation, a tried stone, a precious cornerstone, a sure foundation; whoever believes will not act hastily. Also I will make justice the measuring line, and righteousness the plummet.

Isaiah 28:16–17

Pivotal Point: A woman who builds on a firm foundation will stand.

In fourth grade, I used sugar cubes (tiny blocks of sugar) to build a replica of one of the beautiful old California missions. When the day arrived to take in our projects, I proudly carried mine to school. But when I moved one of my hands from the cardboard foundation to open the door to the school, I dropped my mission, and it broke into pieces. Thankfully, my teacher helped me put the mission back together piece by piece. It didn't look like the original, but my teacher envisioned its prior loveliness and the arduous work that went into creating it. I had worked for weeks, but my masterpiece crumbled in two seconds.

Unlike my fourth-grade project, what God builds endures forever.

Psalm 127:1 tells us, *Unless the Lord builds the house, they labor in vain who build it.*

Hmm. How does God erect the house?

I used cardboard, sugar cubes, and glue to build my California mission. A construction worker uses metal, glass, and wood. But what God builds is greater and much more expansive than any physical structure.

What do you think God is building?

Whether we're framing with steel to create buildings or with love to grow lives, we need God's help. Without it, we'll crumble. Will we allow him? Can we be a pillar? Are we wise women who build what is worthy? Don't answer just yet. First, let's see what we're getting into.

My sugar cube structure fell apart for two reasons:

- It was not built on a stable physical foundation.
- My hands were not steady.

Our spiritual lives are the same way.

What do you think it means to have a stable spiritual foundation?

Matthew 7:24–27 sheds light:

> *Therefore, everyone who hears these words of Mine, and acts on them, will be like a wise man who built his house on the rock. And the rain fell and the floods came, and the winds blew and slammed against that house; and yet it did not fall, for it had been founded on the rock. And everyone who hears these words of Mine, and does not act on them, will be like a foolish man who built his house on the sand. And the rain fell and the floods came, and the winds blew and slammed against that house; and it fell—and its collapse was great* (NASB).

What two types of foundations are compared? Which one lasts? Why did it last? (Hint: the answer is in the first sentence.)

One stood strong. One crashed. With which of these two foundations do you most identify?

As we already talked about in Week Four, storms, hurricane-force winds, drowning in torrential rains, and wading in deep mud, are words we sometimes use to describe our current situation.

When the storm hit, what happened to the person whose house (life) was built on sand (not on the Rock of Jesus)?

How can a collapse affect other areas of our life and bring wide-spread ruin?

The woman who builds wisely digs a deep foundation with a steady hand, creating a sound infrastructure. She monitors her work in progress. She frequently inspects the surroundings. She invests in maintaining the structure.

Inspections, investments, and maintenance are necessary parts of the building process. What do you think this means for our spiritual foundation? How do we inspect and invest and maintain?

Let's talk about two ways.

First, recall Psalm 81:8–16. What does God say in verse 8? Fill in the blank.

Oh that my people would _________________________________ *to me.*

Seriously, let's ask ourselves, *Are we ignoring God?*

How does God identify Himself in this brief passage?

What does God want to do for His people if they choose to listen?

What are the inevitable consequences for those who refuse to listen and obey?

Read John 10:27. Summarize this short but powerful verse.

Are we hearing? Are we striving to listen?

First Kings 17 describes a wild time when Elijah was literally running for his life. He had killed the false prophets and Jezebel wanted to murder him. Elijah was disheartened. The voices in his head had instigated a great big pity party. Eventually, he safely reached a cave in Mt. Horeb. Alone and quiet inside a cave, Elijah heard from God. First Kings 19:11–12 describes the voice:

> *Then he said, "Go out, and stand on the mountain of the LORD."
> And behold, the LORD passed by, and a great and strong wind tore
> into the mountains and broke the rocks in pieces before the LORD,
> but the LORD was not in the wind; and after the wind an
> earthquake, but the LORD was not in the earthquake; and after the
> earthquake a fire, but the Lord was not in the fire; and after the
> fire a still small voice.*

We need to train our ears to identify God's whispers.

Billy Graham once said, "One can approach the Bible with a cold, rationalistic attitude, or one can do so with reverence and the desire to hear God speak." [111]

Second, we need to meditate on God's Word.

We first read Joshua 1:8 in Week Two, Day 1. Let's reread this life-changing verse. What are some synonyms for meditate?

What did the Lord command?

What does the Lord promise?

How would you summarize this verse?

How has meditating on Scripture helped you? Do you think the message and application of this verse is life-changing? Why or why not?

Listen for God's voice, meditate on God's principles, then obey them.

This doesn't imply we won't be broken or fractured at some point. The storms of life are inevitable and could cause collapse and chaos if we're not securely fastened—nailed—to Jesus Christ, the unshakable Rock.

Reflect. Dig deep. Are there any foundational cracks in what you're trying to accomplish?

Now think more broadly. Do you believe our nation's foundation is cracked and crumbling? Why or why not?

How are we contributing to the structure God is building? Proverbs 14:1 tells us, *The wise woman builds her house, but the foolish pulls it down with her hands.* Okay, back to our initial question on the first page of this lesson. Are we wise women who behave as pillars—building up, resisting the urge to tear down? We are when we:

- act on what God says to do (Matthew 7:24–27)
- listen for His voice (Psalm 81:8–16)
- train ourselves (1 Kings 19:11–12)
- meditate on Scripture (Joshua 1:8)

As pillars in our home and community, we are also charged with the responsibly of identifying what's broken or crumbling so we can take action. Let's move to Day 2 where we'll discuss this topic openly and transparently.

What specifically are you choosing to believe from God's Word today?

Day One's Sparkling Gem: I believe I am a pillar, useful and essential in contributing to what God is building.

Prayer: Oh Father, I long to be a pillar—strong and stable, useful, supportable, and uplifting. Provide me with wisdom, and knowledge, and all spiritual understanding so I do not tear apart what You are building. Give me the words to teach this cornerstone concept to other women, not forgetting girls and teens. Help me believe my worth in Your eyes. Give me strength to accept Your value of me. I love You! In Jesus's name, amen.

Perspective: Let's cover our homes in prayer. My friend recently wrote Bible verses on the walls of her new home while it was being constructed. She and her husband buried a Bible behind one of the walls, too. The rest of us, who are not involved in a building project, can write Bible verses on sticky notes and attach them to the walls of our existing house. We can also write special verses on note cards, frame them, and nail them above each room of the house.

Week Five, Day 2

Broken Walls: Don't Lose Heart

God has commissioned us as agents of intervention in the midst of a hostile and
broken world.
Phillip Yancey[112]

*So they took their journey from Succoth and camped in Etham at the edge of the
wilderness. And the Lord went before them by day in a pillar of cloud to lead the
way, and by night in a pillar of fire to give them light, so as to go by day and
night. He did not take away the pillar of cloud by day or the pillar of fire by night
from before the people.*
Exodus 13:20–22

Pivotal Point: A woman with the light of hope eclipses the dark places of
brokenness.

Did you know 10 percent of Americans suffer from depression? And this mood
disorder is increasing in teens and young adults.[113] Some studies disclose that
mental illness is so widespread it outnumbers cancer, diabetes, and heart
disease.[114]

Did you know about 50 percent of married couples in the United States divorce,
the sixth-highest divorce rate in the world? Subsequent marriages have an even
higher divorce rate: 60 percent of second marriages.[115]

Did you know about this article's headline? "Pain in the Nation: U.S. Experienced
Highest Ever Combined Rates of Deaths Due to Alcohol, Drugs, and Suicide
During the First Year of the COVID-19 Pandemic."[116]

Maybe we're not directly affected by divorce, depression, addiction, or suicide,
but unless we're living on a remote island somewhere, we're all indirectly
impacted by their consequences. As God's people, God is preparing us to help. He
is teaching us what we can do.

Sin brought brokenness into the perfect world God created.

The devil uses wicked, broken things in our culture to entice, manipulate, and
separate us from God. Wickedness isn't new. When Paul preached in Ephesus, he

dealt with the pagan worship at the temple of Diana. And Corinth? Sexual debauchery permeated this city. But God's Word still shined through the darkness of idol worship and fleshly perversion.

As we come face to face with broken things of life, we can remember what Paul told the churches in Galatians 6:9–10: *Let us not grow weary while doing good, for in due season we shall reap if we do not lose heart. Therefore, as we have opportunity, let us do good to all, especially to those who are of the household of faith.*

And to Timothy he wrote, *Fight the good fight of faith* (1 Timothy 6:12).

Paul also testified, *We are hard-pressed on every side, yet not crushed; we are perplexed, but not in despair; persecuted, but not forsaken; struck down, but not destroyed ...Therefore we do not lose heart. Even though our outward man is perishing, yet the inward man is being renewed day by day* (2 Corinthians 4:8–9).

Hold on to this hope as we read about broken things and people, specifically the broken walls in Ezekiel 13:3–14. Notice *cause* and *effect*.

> *Woe to the foolish prophets, who follow their own spirit and have seen nothing! O Israel, your prophets are like foxes in the deserts. You have not gone up into the gaps to build a wall for the house of Israel to stand in battle on the day of the LORD. They have envisioned futility and false divination, saying, "Thus says the LORD!" But the LORD has not sent them.*

Now underline the causes and circle the effects in the rest of this passage.

> *Because you have spoken nonsense and envisioned lies, therefore I am indeed against you, says the Lord GOD.*

> *Because they have seduced My people, saying, Peace! when there is no peace—and one builds a wall, and they plaster it with untempered mortar—say to those who plaster it with untempered mortar, that it will fall.*

> *So I will break down the wall you have plastered with untempered mortar, and bring it down to the ground, so that its foundation will be uncovered; it will fall, and you shall be consumed in the midst of it.*

These crumbling walls symbolize our broken mentalities, beliefs, morals, and convictions.

Maybe you skipped over the phrase *untempered mortar* (v.10).

Untempered mortar was also called, *sorry stuff.*[117] Interesting.

This *sorry stuff* is symbolic of what foolish prophets or deceivers used to construct spiritual walls and offered no protection against the enemy and no strength against the onslaught of life. The mortar, though, was like using sand without lime, or mud without straw. Both were useless and could not bind or hold the bricks of a defensive wall together. So, in fact, the untempered mortar only gave the appearance of strength and beauty, yet the wall was actually weak and ready to fall.

This is intriguing.

Something about this passage is familiar.

Think of instances of brokenness in our homes, communities, nation, or world. How do we whitewash them, making them seem all right—even, functioning, or beautiful?

In the Ezekiel 13 passage, the New American Standard Bible uses *whitewash* in place of "untempered mortar." Maybe this word is more familiar.

Jesus uses this word in Matthew 23:27 when He says, *"Woe to you, scribes and Pharisees, hypocrites! For you are like whitewashed tombs which indeed appear beautiful outwardly, but inside are full of dead men's bones and all uncleanness."*

Outwardly attractive, but inwardly vile.

Whitewashing. Using untempered mortar or sorry stuff—making evil seem not so bad. But evil's wicked foundation is destined to crumble.

Today the Ezekiel message reveals a crisis: the lies we accept or the truth we ignore will eventually bring destruction.

What lie(s) does Hollywood make attractive but at its core has no substance or worth?

Crafty and cunning as foxes, the false prophets schemed to deceive God's people by misrepresenting or twisting God's words. The devil uses the same strategy. His clever seduction shouts, "Did God really say that?" Same spiel he gave Adam and Eve (Genesis 3:1).

What lies are some politicians pushing as truth? What beliefs have become unsteady, blurred, or normalized?

In what ways has our culture whitewashed God's truth and indoctrinated our students?

What is one way you are negatively affected by our culture's values, laws, regulations, or expected norms?

What is a lie Satan is whitewashing over our children and young people today?

What do you think has changed so that some children have little or no knowledge of the Bible? What has replaced their family devotions or church?

Describe how each of the following could contribute to a broken society:

Lack of godly parental influence:

Lack of appropriate discipline:

Worldly entertainment:

Lack of self-respect, poor self-image:

The need for acceptance:

These questions might provoke anger, even compel us to point fingers and issue blame.

Actually, who *is* to blame?

Ephesians 6:12 tells us, *We do not wrestle against flesh and blood, but against principalities, against powers, against the rulers of the darkness of this age, against spiritual hosts of wickedness in the heavenly places.*

Based on this Scripture, who is our enemy?

As a result, we may feel overwhelmed, sad, or helpless. But we don't have to be crippled by any of these factors.

You might wonder. How? Where is the hope that breaks through the darkness of evil?

The Light of Hope was switched on thousands of years ago. Isaiah 53:5 tells us:

> *But He was wounded for our transgressions, He was bruised for*
> *our iniquities; the chastisement for our peace was upon Him, and*
> *by His stripes we are healed.*

This passage prophesized God's plan for Jesus to make a way for restoration. Healing broken people, families, communities, and nations is God's idea, His heart, and His strength.

> *Those from among you shall build the old waste places; You shall*
> *raise up the foundations of many generations; and you shall be*
> *called the Repairer of the Breach, The Restorer of Streets to Dwell*
> *In* (Isaiah 58:12).

Repairer of the Breach. Restorer of Streets to Dwell In.

These are beautiful names for God.

At the time of this writing, the entertainment at the 2023 Grammy Awards program featured a filthy, unholy, satanic-like performance. But also during this timeframe, a weeklong revival broke out at Asbury University in Kentucky.

Repairer. Restorer. God continues to raise up courageous men and women to tear down what's wicked and rebuild what's worthwhile.

As pillars we have a responsibility to say *no* to the lies.

As pillars we uphold God's truth.

As pillars we shine the hope of Jesus.

Our mission begins at home, then shines into the community, nation, and ultimately impacts the world.

So gather around the table and feast on the hope and healing found in Jesus Christ. In next week's study, we'll talk about how we can actively participate in what God is doing.

Your shining beams are slicing through darkness. I can see them from here.

What specifically are you choosing to believe from God's Word today?

Day Two's Sparkling Gem: I believe I am a pillar of God's truth, upholding my family and community.

Prayer: Oh Restorer of the Streets, my heart sinks with sadness at the destruction openly taking place in our families, communities, and nation. I am grieved by the lies, false beauty, and the alluring pull of evil, just as You are grieved. But, God, I know You win! We win! You are on the throne, and nothing is out of Your sight. I am grateful I have Your strength to make a difference in those around me. Help me be bold. Show me the best way to make a difference today. In Jesus's name, amen.

Perspective: A favorite space in the house can be the kitchen table where we're invited to enjoy delicious food, conversation, and laughter. Gather your friends—four pillars make a strong support—and commit to pray for one another. Then brainstorm practical ways your group can be agents of intervention in a broken world.

Week Five, Day 3

Standing in the Gap

For we are but a vapor and we have to make it count. We're on. Direct us, Lord,
and get us on our feet.
Beth Moore[118]

*He who overcomes, I will make him a pillar in the temple of My God, and he shall
go out no more. I will write on him the name of My God and the name of the city
of My God, the New Jerusalem, which comes down out of heaven from My God.
And I will write on him My new name.*

Revelation 3:12

Pivotal Point: A woman with a battle plan can stand in the gap.

Maybe you've been running a mile a minute. You dream about a nap. You're not
alone. One study found 53 percent of women say they're worn out.[119]

Relax. *Standing in the gap* doesn't mean you must stand. Sitting or kneeling could
be better.

In the last chapter, we discussed lies that lead to broken people, homes, and
communities. Whitewashing over deception is a common, expected practice. In
fact, darkness is sometimes celebrated or worshipped.

Let's revisit Ezekiel 13:3–5: *Thus says the Lord God: "Woe to the foolish
prophets, who follow their own spirit and have seen nothing! O Israel, your
prophets are like foxes in the deserts.* **You have not gone up into the gaps** *to
build a wall for the house of Israel to stand in battle on the day of the Lord*
(emphasis mine).

In ancient times, a wall protected the city. A hole or gap in the wall made physical
space for the enemy to infiltrate and invade. The same is true in our spiritual lives.
When we let down our guard, disbelieve, have selfish thoughts, or listen to lies,
the devil can slither through the cracks and hammer our broken spirit.

When something is broken, we need a plan for repair. If there's a hole in the wall
of our house, we make a renovation plan quickly. We don't want anything that
slithers, nibbles, or swarms coming through the crevices. A hole left unattended

201

could mean an invasion of rodents or termites that destroy the foundation, causing our house to fall.

Ezekiel 22:30 tells us:

> *So I sought for a man among them who would make a wall, and stand in the gap before Me on behalf of the land, that I should not destroy it;* **but I found no one** *(emphasis mine).*

God says He is seeking someone to stand in the gap. What do you think this position requires?

Another time, God found a person to stand in the gap:

> *Therefore He said that He would destroy them, if Moses, His chosen one, had not stood in the gap before Him, to turn away His wrath from destroying them* (Psalm 106:23 NASB).

Our communities and nations are in dangerous times.

Like Moses, we've been created, strengthened, set apart, and positioned to stand, sit, or kneel, and intercede for our children, family, neighbors, and leaders. We stand in the gap when we pray for:

- those in a crisis situation
- people who don't know God, don't believe in Him, or are angry at Him
- individuals living in opposition to God's Word
- political leaders focused on establishing destructive social laws
- those who comprise unjust governments
- people who are weak, hurt, and abandoned
- those entangled in occult practices
- people engaged in immoral conduct
- anyone enslaved to addictions
- those who need to be protected
- organizations who omit God and create their own gods

There is much to pray about!

Lamentations 2:19 tells us, *Arise, cry out in the night, at the beginning of the watches; pour out your heart like water before the face of the Lord. Lift your hands toward Him for the life of your young children, who faint from hunger at the head of every street.*

And Nehemiah 4:14 says, *And I looked, and arose and said to the nobles, to the leaders, and to the rest of the people, "Do not be afraid of them. Remember the Lord, great and awesome, and fight for your brethren, your sons, your daughters, your wives, and your houses.*

As pillars we can boldly respond to evil and injustice, and fight for innocent children. Based on the verses above, what can we do? Circle all that apply.

    arise   wait   watch   remember

    cry out   sleep   fight   ignore

    lift your hands   pour out your heart

What do you think it means to fight for the people we love?

What do you think it means to remember God? Why does this matter?

Why do you think we're instructed to lift our hands?

Dictionaries offer many definitions of *power* including "the ability to act or produce an effect."[120] As Christ-followers, we have access to the most powerful weapons designed to destroy what's viciously attacking our families and leaders in our community.

Our powerful weapon is two-fold:

- Prayer
- God's Word—the Sword of the Spirit

First, prayer can flip the upside down to upright. By prayer, circumstances are altered, outcomes are changed, minds are transformed, hearts are mended, and people are marvelously transported from darkness into the marvelous light of God's truth.

Second, reading the Bible reveals who God is and what His plans are. The Bible uncovers His character and exposes His faithfulness, which instills in us confidence, faith, and trust. The Bible gives instruction and guidance, provides knowledge and wisdom, and lavishes hope on our weary souls.

Recall Hebrews 12:4:

> *For the word of God is living and powerful, and sharper than any two-edged sword, piercing even to the division of soul and spirit, and of joints and marrow, and is a discerner of the thoughts and intents of the heart.*

Have you seen a two-edged sword? Can you grasp the damage it can do? With blades on either side, no matter how you turn it, it cuts. Likewise, the Word of God does it's intended job and will prevail.

Revisit a question from the last chapter: What do you think is the greatest danger facing our children today?

What do you think women need protection from?

How can we stand in the gap and pray for our men?

The devil strives to keep us busy or distracted so our time in the Bible will be limited, or non-existent. The devil is fully aware of a truth some of us don't believe: the more time we spend in the Bible, the more powerful and victorious we'll become—a force to be reckoned with.

Here Is Your Battle Plan

Take a look at this encouraging and powerful battle plan. Girl, it will pump us up!

Nehemiah hears the distressing news that the wall in Jerusalem is broken down and its gates are burned with fire (Nehemiah 1:3).

A huge problem. At this time in history, a city without a wall was like a house without a door. The enemy could surely invade. Nehemiah, like all of us, had options. He could ignore the problem, blame others, or take action.

Let's read Nehemiah 1:1–11 again.

What five things did Nehemiah do in verse four?

He _______________ (opposite of stand).

He _______________ (released from tear ducts).

He _______________ (opposite of rejoiced).

He _______________ (instead of eating).

He _______________ (what God commands us to do).

Nehemiah emptied himself. Then he prayed. His prayer is recorded in Nehemiah 1:5–11.

How did he identify God? (v. 5)

What does he ask God to do? (v. 6)

What does he seek forgiveness from? (v. 7)

What does Nehemiah wholeheartedly believe God can do? (vv. 8–9)

Again, how does he identify God? What does he ask Him to do? (vv. 10–11).

In God's providence, Nehemiah was positioned, equipped, and courageous. He boldly prayed to God believing He would listen. Then with full power and authority, He would act.

Onward to a spectacular outcome in Nehemiah 2:2–10.

Whom did Nehemiah approach? What did he ask him? (vv. 2–5).

What was the king's response? (v. 8)

Nehemiah *believed* God.

Might I add, for the sake of being greatly astonished, Nehemiah 6:15 tells us the wall was rebuilt in only fifty-two days. Yeah. He's our God.

Nehemiah's victorious battle plan is suitable for every decision and for every prayer.

Maybe you're praying about a work situation for yourself or another person. The outcome isn't dependent on whether your co-worker, colleague, or boss is a believer. The outcome hinges on God's perfect will and our eternal good. His plan can't be thwarted.

Your boss? Leader? Family member? They may never understand why they've changed their mind, went another direction, or found favor with you. But God used them to bring about change and fulfill His purpose.

Our prayers may result in an outcome that looks different than what we envisioned. Or they may appear unanswered in our lifetime. But we can know with 100 percent surety that when God's power is unleashed, victory follows.

Recall the phrase back in Week One Priscilla Shirer used: *courageously thriving.*

Standing in the gap requires courage. Connect with other pillars—your sisters in Christ. A single pillar can't support the roof on a house, but four pillars can. Likewise, when we advocate for and with one another, we're capable of being *the light of the world. A city that is set on a hill cannot be hidden* (Matthew 5:14).

Keep your lamp burning. Let's move to Day 4 for specific prayers to pray.

What specifically are you choosing to believe from God's Word today?

Day Three's Sparkling Gem: I believe I am a pillar, and my artillery authorizes me to stand in the gap.

Prayer: Mighty Commander, I'm fighting a battle. But I know I will be victorious. I bow before You now. Give me guidance. Show me what to do, how to handle this situation. Give me words to speak and confidence to act. You know the details and know the end result. I praise You, God, for Your involvement. In Jesus's name, amen.

Perspective: Return to Nehemiah's prayer in Nehemiah 1:5–11. Write this prayer down and use it as a model prayer to be prayed regularly or when your own words won't come so easily.

Front-Door Protection and Roof-Top Prayers

*Through my prayers I can change the destiny of a life. I don't move a muscle,
but I help move the hand of God.*
Joni Eareckson Tada[121]

*Confess your trespasses to one another, and pray for one another, that you may
be healed. The effective, fervent prayer of a righteous man avails much. Elijah
was a man with a nature like ours, and he prayed earnestly that it would not rain;
and it did not rain on the land for three years and six months. And he prayed
again, and the heaven gave rain, and the earth produced its fruit.*
James 5:16–18

Pivotal point: A woman in prayer transforms people everywhere.

"Whatcha doing, Mom?"

Wearing footed pajamas, my two-and-a-half-year-old climbed off his big-boy
bed, crept down the stairs into the hallway, and peered into the quiet, dimly lit
kitchen. Sitting in a corner chair, Bible open on my lap, I was meeting with
God—my regular 5:30 a.m. morning habit.

"Praying," I responded.

He slowly inquired, "Are yew prayin' for me?"

I smiled and said, "I am."

That was twenty-five years ago.

Today, I linger in the same space, in the same kitchen, in the same beloved house.
And I continue to pray the same prayer, for this boy, who is now a man.

Sometimes, in the early morning when it's still dark and I'm reading my Bible
only by the light from my teapot lamp, I envision him, his sleepy little face,
looking around the corner of the hall into the kitchen. Immediately, I'm prompted
to pray.

What's your gut reaction to this question: Do you believe in prayer? We'll come back to that question later.

For now, we'll explore how prayer brings healing to brokenness and revolutionizes our homes and communities.

According to a recent survey, 55 percent of adults said they pray daily. [122] To whom they pray wasn't revealed. Only a little more than half—68 percent—of self-identified Christians say they pray regularly.

Why do you think many Christ-followers neglect prayer?

Colossians 4:2 says, *Continue earnestly in prayer, being vigilant in it with thanksgiving.*

Pause on the word *vigilant*.

The Merriam-Webster's Dictionary defines vigilant this way: "alertly watchful especially to avoid danger." Synonyms include watchful, wide-awake, intense, unremitting, and alert. "Alert stresses readiness or promptness in meeting danger or in seizing opportunity."[123]

Probing for an open door, a crack, a gap, an entrance without a watchman, the devil conspires to rip apart our children, like a lion devours his prey. He begins with their minds.

Counter attack.

Stay watchful of trends, laws, and shifting attitudes, and vigilantly pray against the evil explicitly invading.

Before we proceed, we need to come face-to-face with what we believe about prayer.

How often do you pray?

What do you pray about?

How satisfied are you with your prayer life?

What, if anything, keeps you from spending time in prayer? Circle any that apply.

Distractions   Unbelief   Guilt   Other priorities

Don't know how   Other_____________________

When we communicate with God through prayer, Satan knows he'll be stripped of all his power over us, so he cleverly uses a variety of tools and methods to ensure we don't do what we intended.

Once, I was beginning to pray in my quiet living room. I got down on my knees and had only uttered a few words when I opened my eyes and saw a Christmas ornament under the sofa from the previous year. Then I noticed the dust! My first impulse was to clean.

Really? Anything… anything at all to distract.

The answer may appear obvious at first glance, but for the sake of seeing it in writing, how does busyness inhibit prayer?

In what ways does guilt and shame deter prayer?

How does unbelief determine our attitude toward prayer?

Do you sometimes think God is unwilling to answer prayers? Why or why not?

Let's trek through God's Word on a prayer excursion. First, we'll talk about *How to Approach God* and then *Prayers for Children/Loved Ones.*

How to Approach God

    1.   Approach God with the respect He is worthy of.

The passage in 1 Chronicles 29:11–13 is a powerful description. What does this passage reveal about God?

I often want to share this favorite scripture passage. But inevitably, I forget the reference or invert the numbers. Finally, I associated the 1 Chronicles 29:11 reference with Jeremiah 29:11:

> *For I know the thoughts that I think toward you, says the LORD,*
> *thoughts of peace and not of evil, to give you a future and a hope.*

Now I can remember each verse is 29:11. It then occurred to me that our purpose as pillars begins with knowing God.

What do the following passages say about approaching God?

Matthew 6:9–10

Psalm 95:2

2.   Approach God with confidence.

Although He is holy, God invites us into His presence. What do the following
scriptures say about approaching God?

Hebrews 4:16

Isaiah 65:24

Jeremiah 32:17, 27

Psalm 5:3

Philippians 4:6–7

3.   Approach God with a clean heart.

Satan's goal is to separate us from God. He hammers condemnation and shame, so we'll hide from God as Adam and Eve attempted to do in the garden of Eden. God's conviction isn't intended to push us away; it's meant to turn us around and draw us back to Him. He loves us so much. What do these scripture passages or verses say?

Mark 11:24–25

Psalm 66:18

1 Samuel 12:23

Take a few moments and ask God to reveal any sin hampering your relationship with Him. What do you think He's showing you?

4. Approach God with your unique voice.

- Pray naturally.

Your relationship with God is as unique as you are. Use words you're comfortable with to express yourself. A sophisticated vocabulary isn't necessary. Language doesn't determine whether a prayer is wimpy or powerful. It's the attitude and confidence behind the words, and the belief in the One to whom we're praying that determines a prayer's effectiveness. Rambling rhetoric is useless when the speaker doubts God's power or interest. Conversely, "help me" uttered with sincere humility causes God to incline His ear. [124]

- Pray transparently.

Pray as sincerely and honestly as you know how. Tell God everything. He made you and knows everything about you: your thoughts, beliefs, and fears. You won't surprise Him. His mercy, grace, love, and forgiveness are limitless.

- Pray often.

First Thessalonians 5:17 tells us, *Pray without ceasing.*

To pray continually doesn't imply we pray every moment. Rather, praying frequently and persistently keeps us in an attitude of prayer. Dependence on God, then, becomes a lifestyle that reflects gratitude.

- Listen.

Listen for God to speak to your spirit as you read His Word. Pay attention to His gentle nudges when you pray. Reflect on God's past faithfulness. These are ways God speaks to us.

5.   Eliminate distractions.

Praying throughout the day while working, shopping, waiting, or driving in the car, is a persistent attitude of prayer. But in these settings, there are also distractions and interruptions.

Include secluded, quiet, intentional prayer.

Luke 5:16 tells us, *He [Jesus]Himself often withdrew into the wilderness and prayed.*

Create a wilderness place to pray. Get up early or stay up late.

Put Psalm 109:4 on your calendar or on our daily list of things to do: *But I am in prayer* (NASB).

Let's go! Let's pray.

Prayers for Children/ Loved Ones

Praying for our children and loved ones is a never-ending privilege. Likely, others aren't praying for your special people like you are. Investing time in communication with God is worth the effort. When prayed-over children exit the home, they impact their communities, which ultimately influences the nation.

The Bible is packed full of verses we can pray over our children and adults. Numerous books have been written exclusively on this topic. For this short study, however, let's focus on five passages or verses.

Write the name of the person for whom you are praying in the blank.

The first prayer is based on Colossians 1:9–14.

> Loving Father,
> Thank you for _______________. I am grateful You love them even more than I do.
> I pray _________________ will know Your specific plan for her/his life. May ___________________'s conversation, character, and conduct, reveal obedience to You. I pray _______________________________ will live in a manner worthy of Jesus Christ. I pray ______________________________bear the fruit of the spirit and influence the world one person at a time. I pray __________________ will

study the Bible, apply what it says, and grow closer to You every day. I pray he/she will recognize the connection between his/her decisions to obey and disobey You and the consequences or blessings that result. I pray _____________________ will realize his/her helplessness and rely on Your strength. I pray _____________________ will remember to give thanks to You and to trust You. I pray that hardships will develop a deeper character. In the name of Jesus, I pray.

Our second prayer comes from 2 Timothy 1:7. We studied this verse in Week Two, Day 1. Recall that a sound mind means clarity, not confusion.

> Powerful, Holy God,
> Remove fear and give _____________________ power
> and love and a clear mind without any confusion. In Jesus's name, amen.

Our third prayer is modeled after King David's prayer for his son, Solomon, as he prepared to build the temple. God has a plan and purpose for the person for whom you are praying. *These things* in this verse refer to the things God has planned. Let's pray 1 Chronicles 29:19 over our loved ones.

> Almighty God,
> Give _____________________ a loyal heart to keep Your
> commandments and Your testimonies and Your statutes, to do all these
> things. In Your name, amen.

The fourth prayer comes from Psalm 119:18.

> Lord and Savior,
> Open _____________________'s eyes, so he /she may see
> wondrous things from Your law. In Jesus's name, amen.

Our last prayer comes from Psalm 20:4.

> Dearest Jesus,
> Give _____________________ his/her heart's desire, and fulfill
> all _____________________'s purpose. In Jesus's name, amen.

We might not recognize the extent of what our prayers have accomplished or what our prayers have protected our loved ones from. Never abandon your prayers or mistakenly believe God doesn't care. He does.

Recall the opening question on page one: Do you believe prayer makes a difference?

Refer to the quote by Joni Eareckson Tada at the beginning of this lesson. In your own words, write what you think she means. How will you apply her perspective to your prayers today?

Stand at the door with the sword of truth drawn. Climb to the rooftop and shout His praise. You are a shining light, a pillar standing on truth (1 Timothy 3:15).

What specifically are you choosing to believe from God's Word today?

Day Four's Sparkling Gem: I believe my prayers transform lives.

Prayer: Oh Father, thank You for the relationship I have with You and for the privilege of being able to boldly come to the throne of grace to receive Your help and mercy. Help me believe I might be the only one praying for the people most precious and special to me—my children, my family, my loved ones. Help me remember to add daily secluded prayer to my list of things to do, because prayer is important. Thank You, God for caring about me and my loved ones. In Jesus's name, amen.

Perspective: Gather small tin-can type containers, suitable as ornaments for the Christmas tree and conceal notes inside them. I've written prayers over the decades for each of my children and for my husband, too. Then at Christmas you can reread your prayers. Some will be answered, perhaps differently than imagined. Others are in progress. Either way, these ornaments make special gifts and are a legacy of prayer.

Week Five, Day 5

Leave the Light On

The greatest legacy one can pass on to one's children and grandchildren is not
money … but rather a legacy of character and faith.
Billy Graham[125]

*You shall love the Lord your God with all your heart, with all your soul, and with
all your strength. And these words which I command you today shall be in your
heart. You shall teach them diligently to your children, and shall talk of them
when you sit in your house, when you walk by the way, when you lie down, and
when you rise up. You shall bind them as a sign on your hand, and they shall be
as frontlets between your eyes. You shall write them on the doorposts of your
house and on your gates.*
Deuteronomy 6:5–9

Pivotal Point: A woman who reflects God leaves a shining legacy.

In lieu of flowers at my husband's memorial, more than $7,000.00 dollars was
donated to erect a playground for the Pandita Ramabai Mukti Mission in
Kedgaon, a village located forty miles east of the city of Pune, in the Republic of
India. Approximately 250 orphans are cared for at the mission, and 2,500 students
either walk or travel by bus to attend the mission's school. At the dedication of
that playground, the US Mukti Mission Executive Director said to the children,
"When you play on the Alan Presnell Memorial Playground, remember Alan was
a man who loved God and loved his wife."

My husband was a fierce protector, especially of children. His legacy of love
extended 10,000 miles to the other side of the world. Knowing the children are
joyfully playing and laughing would make him joyful, too.

Some think of legacy as a gift of money or personal property. In fact, these
synonyms are often interchanged with legacy: birthright, heritage, inheritance,
and bequest.

Legacy can also reflect our values, attitudes, and beliefs. My husband's gift was
more than a physical structure; it represented his morals and love for God.

One dictionary expands *legacy's* meaning: "The long-lasting impact of particular events, and actions that took place in the past, or of a person's life." One example they provide is, "Future generations will be left with a legacy of pollution and destruction." [126]

Polluted or not, we choose the kind of legacy we leave.

Throughout this study, we've read about several women who sowed seeds of love and courage and created lasting legacies:

- Queen Esther boldly acted and prevented annihilation for the Hebrews.
- Jochebed saved Moses' life when she resisted fear and obeyed God.
- Midwives Puah and Shiphuah bravely did what was right.
- Influential Priscilla pioneered one of the first churches in the Roman Empire.
- Prostitute Rehab's choice made her the ancestor of Jesus.
- Infertile Hannah gave birth to Samuel, the prophet.
- Mary poured expensive perfume on Jesus's head, and she's remembered for her grateful, generous act.

Hmm. What seeds am I sowing? What am I leaving in the world?

I want to leave the kind of fragrance this person was talking about:

> Death is never the last word on the life of a man. When a man leaves the world, be he righteous or unrighteous, he leaves something in the world. He may leave something that will grow and spread like a cancer or a poison, or he may leave something like the fragrance of perfume or a blossom of beauty that permeates the atmosphere with blessing. [127]

A beautiful fragrance is possible when we believe God—what He says about Himself and what He says about us. Believing God, then, empowers us to sow seeds into the next generation and leave a legacy that permeates the atmosphere,

Let's look together at 2 Corinthians 4:1–6. The passage, though not a typical perspective about legacy, can shape our attitudes and help us recognize our purpose.

> *Therefore, since we have this ministry, as we have received mercy, we do not lose heart. But we have renounced the hidden things of shame, not walking in craftiness nor handling the word of God deceitfully, but by manifestation of the truth commending ourselves*

Why is it vital to sow seeds?

> *But even if our gospel is veiled, it is veiled to those who are perishing, whose minds the god of this age has blinded, who do not believe, lest the light of the gospel of the glory of Christ, who is the image of God, should shine on them. For we do not preach ourselves, but Christ Jesus the Lord, and ourselves your bondservants for Jesus' sake. For it is the God who commanded light to shine out of darkness, who has shone in our hearts to give the light of the knowledge of the glory of God in the face of Jesus Christ.*

Digging deeper into this passage is insightful. For clarification, I've emphasized significant words and paraphrased the verses to clarify their application:

As strong, beautiful, wise, refined pillars, we have a **ministry** on earth and God's mercy is on our life. Because of His mercy, we're not discouraged (v. 1).

His strength enables us to renounce shame and deception and watered-down truth for the purpose of gaining favor from those who don't believe. God's **truth is our conscience** and beautiful in His sight (v. 2).

The gospel is veiled because of **unbelief, which diminishes the light.** However, when we walk like we **believe Jesus, we naturally shine** (v. 3).

Those who mock the Savior and **refuse to believe Him are spiritually blind.** They are as the "walking dead" **unable to see the light** of the gospel. Reflecting the image of God, we're able to **shine** God's love to the lost (v. 4).

Jesus preached. We can **talk, share,** and **demonstrate** God's love (v. 5).

God commanded "light to shine from darkness." The God who created natural light now shines in our hearts. **His light in our hearts gives light to others** (v. 6).

This. Is. Our. Legacy!

No matter our title, who we hang out with, where we live, or where we've come from, the way in which we accept the Light and point others to Him is the greatest legacy of all.

Oh, girl, this is so good!

There are countless ways to shine the light and infuse a sweet fragrant legacy. I've started a list.

- Tell your story. Keep a journal. Write an autobiography or memoir. Psalm 145:4 tells us, *One generation shall praise Your works to another, and shall declare Your mighty acts.*

- Pass on your knowledge. Write a blog. Teach or mentor others, especially the younger generation.

- Continue family traditions. Write notes, take photographs, and share heirlooms. Psalm 78:4 says, *We will not hide them from their children, telling to the generation to come the praises of the LORD, and His strength and His wonderful works that He has done.*

- Pass along your skills, talents, and abilities.

- Volunteer and serve others.

- Share your faith-building lessons. Second Timothy 1:5 says, *I am reminded of your sincere faith, a faith that dwelt first in your grandmother Lois and your mother Eunice and now, I am sure, dwells in you as well* (ESV).

- Love. Teach others how to love. Psalm 103:17 tells us, *But the steadfast love of the LORD is from everlasting to everlasting on those who fear him, and his righteousness to children's children* (ESV).

- Live a meaningful life with integrity. Proverbs 20:7 says, *The righteous man walks in his integrity; his children are blessed after him.*

What ideas do you have?

Joanna Gaines (*The Magnolia Story*) said, "Don't quit, and don't give up. The reward is just around the corner. And in times of doubt or times of joy, listen for that still, small voice. Know that God has been there from the beginning—and he will be there until . . . The End."[128]

Don't quit.

Don't give up.

What is the still, small voice saying to you about the impact you can begin making or the current one(s) you are?

Jesus said in Matthew 5:13, *You are the salt of the earth.*

We know that salt adds flavor and as salt you flavor those around you and even those who aren't—like the way my husband did in India. Don't be shy about this next question. Your inspiration and desire to make a difference is God-given. What are some legacy-building activities that you are currently involved in?

Second Timothy 2:21 tells us, *[She] will be a vessel for honor, sanctified and useful for the Master, prepared for every good work.*

Sanctification comes from the Greek word *hagiosmo* and means "set apart" for God's purpose.[129]

This is what we do as pillars—we are set apart to boldly reflect the Light. His purpose and plan for us is to unfold a shining legacy.

What does your life symbolize? In what way(s) do you feel set apart for an extraordinary legacy?

Life and legacy occur simultaneously:

- ✓ Your character comprised of the fruit of the Spirit bubbles out of you.
- ✓ Your faith in God dictates your actions.
- ✓ Your humility results in strength and enables you to live out your purpose with clear focus.
- ✓ Your inner beauty draws others to you, and then they see Him.
- ✓ Your wisdom, knowledge, teaching, and training are ways you impart truth to others.
- ✓ Your trust is in God and is evident in trials.
- ✓ Your service to your family, church, and community is serving God.
- ✓ Your generosity with time and finances bring Him glory.
- ✓ Your compassionate care of others reflects the grace and care God has shown you.

My husband's light is still on—even though his earthly body is gone. And our light will be too. Remember, *You are the light of the world. A city that is set on a hill cannot be hidden* (Matthew 5:14).

Shine, girl. Just shine!

Next week we'll gather for one last time and discuss one of the most practical ways to shine.

What specifically are you choosing to believe from God's Word today?

Day Five's Sparkling Gem: I believe my faith and actions are launching a shining legacy.

Prayer: Father, I thank You for my ministry and the strength and courage You've given me to believe. I thank You for your truth and for enabling me to naturally shine. I pray for my spiritually blind family and friends who are unable to see the Light. Help me to shine in a way so their eyes are opened, and they see You. Teach me to use my words for Your glory. Give me strength to share. Give me boldness to demonstrate the true light. In Jesus's name, amen.

Perspective: If you haven't already done so, create a scrapbook. In it describes yourself and what you believe. Include favorite Bible verses, photos, and recipes, and any other information you'd want others to know about you.

Participant's Guide

Our identity is not a

____ revelation.

This woman is ____________________________.

The Bible says in Luke 12:12, *The Holy Spirit will teach you in that very hour what* ____________________________.

<u>**Conclusion: Week Six—She Shines**</u>

View Conclusion:
Week Six Video on YouTube:

I'm glad you're here for our final week. I've loved spending time with you, and I don't want to say goodbye.

Shining the light on Psalm 144:12 has solidified my identity in Jesus Christ and empowered me as His daughter. I'm confident our time together has been an empowering experience for you, too. Because when we place the spotlight on God's Word and invest time with Him—questioning, seeking, meditating, and believing—there's no conceivable way to remain the same.

Our identity, though, is not a one and done revelation. I mean, at least for us. From God's perspective, when we place our faith in Him, we are His—forever.

But to maintain the joy and belief in our identity we need to spend time with God every day … gathering truth like fresh manna. Collecting and plucking them from the Bible.

God knows we need this.

James 1:22–24 tells us,

> *Do not merely listen to the word, and so deceive yourselves. Do what it says. Anyone who listens to the word but does not do what it says is like someone who looks at his face in a mirror. And, after looking at himself, goes away and immediately forgets what he looks like.*

So, with eyes wide open, we gaze into God's Holy Word, and meditate on truth.

We ruminate on that very thing God has showed us. We say, I believe.

> *I believe* God's words and His perspective.
> *I believe* God designed me and I am of great value.
> *I believe* God has a plan and purpose for me.

I believe I am filled with the Holy Spirit and therefore strengthened and
courageous.
I believe I am fashioned in the image of Christ and therefore beautiful.
I believe walking with Him daily cultivates internal beauty.
I believe discernment enables me to hold truth and discard lies.
I believe wisdom shapes my mindset and attitude.
I believe I am polished and purified in the fires of refinement.
I believe I am a pillar fit for a palace within my home, community, and
nation.
I believe I am building a legacy of God's love.

Thank You, God, for revealing the truth.

Your truth, like a magnifier reflecting the sun, sets a fire that burns bright within
us.

Your truth provides life-altering principles that dispel the myths and remind us of
who we are in Christ.

No …

We are not among the millions of women still trying to figure out how God views
a woman.

Rather, we embrace our beauty and our womanhood in Christ Jesus.

Don't you just love being a woman—a woman who recognizes God's perspective,
design, and purpose?

In the introduction to this study, you were challenged to:

- *think* differently, more decisively, more consistently
- *see* yourself through another lens
- *say* what you wish you had known
- *feel* invigorated and enthusiastic
- *smell* the sweet aroma of a confirmed or validated identity in Christ
- *hear* God's loving voice
- *act* on new convictions

Well, it's time to act.

During our time together we talked about Esther, Puah, Shiphuah, Jochebed, Abigail, Priscilla, Rahab, Mary of Bethany, Martha, Mary (mother of Jesus), and Hannah. Radiant women who changed everything. Another radiant woman is about to share her story.

This woman is *you.*

And *your story* is remarkable.

One of the best ways we can shine the light in a murky world is by sharing the gospel through our own stories. Your story might be your conversion with a dramatic before and after. It could be a single event or experience. Maybe it's about the moment you recognized God was pursuing you. Regardless, when did God show up? What did He do to change your life? What hope did He pour out? The answer to these questions *is* your story.

On the next few pages, I'll take you through some simple steps so you can talk about the hope we have in Jesus with freedom, confidence, and spontaneity.

How comfortable are you talking about Jesus? Does this thought provoke fear or anxiety?

Do you feel inadequate? Afraid you'll mess up, say the wrong thing, or not know what to say at all?

I get it. I used to feel these same emotions. But don't worry. You won't mess up. Even if you only say, "Jesus loves you," you have spoken truth.

But here's even more truth and hope for you. The Bible says in Luke 12:12, *The Holy Spirit will teach you in that very hour what you ought to say.*

Whew.

Not dependent on our language or intelligence.

But the Holy Spirit's leading. Is there any other way?

Hey, I'm the worst at remembering Scripture references. And maybe you are too. But that's okay. Sometimes a lack of remembrance incites curiosity and provokes a deeper dive. You and the person with whom you are sharing can search the Bible together.

So, relax. Breathe.

But you wonder … *My story is personal. Why is it important to talk about it?*

We share our stories with others so they too can know our faithful and marvelous Lord and Savior. Matthew 28:18–20 tells us:

> *Go therefore and make disciples of all the nations, baptizing them*
> *in the name of the Father and of the Son and of the Holy Spirit,*
> *teaching them to observe all things that I have commanded you;*
> *and lo, I am with you always, even to the end of the age." Amen.*

And Jesus said in Mark 16:15, *Go into all the world and preach the gospel to every creature.*

So we go.

And we tell.

Then we shine the light of God's truth and break through the veil of darkness. Like a million flickering diamonds against a pitch-black backdrop, we shine.

Week Six, Day 1

Your Story: Shining the Light for Greatest Impact

Don't shine so others can see you. Shine so that through you, others can see Him.
C. S. Lewis[130]

You yourselves are our letter, written on our hearts, known and read by everyone. You show that you are a letter from Christ, the result of our ministry, written not with ink but with the Spirit of the living God, not on tablets of stone but on tablets of human hearts.
2 Corinthians 3:2–3

Pivotal Point: God empowers His daughters to share the Light of the gospel.

"Mom don't say anything," my ten-year-old son pleaded.

We were at a popular summer festival when we heard a man shouting through a bullhorn. Bullhorn Billy is the name I gave him.

My young son took hold of my arm to pull me in the other direction.

I responded, "I won't." At my son's urging we moved on.

Bullhorn Billy was bellowing spiritual truths, yet his condemning stance pushed me (and others) away. He didn't know me, my need, or my story. He stood on a platform. He shouted *sinner* and *repentance*. No one slowed down to ask questions. He never made eye contact.

Have you ever seen anything like this? What are some ways you've seen the gospel preached or shared outside of church?

Why do you think Bullhorn Billy's message wasn't received?

Do you think resistance is human nature? Why or why not?

If you have ever had an encounter like this, did you feel judged or embarrassed? Why or why not?

My son and I meandered down the street. To my left stood a large outdoor pavilion. The people were friendly and offered my son and I bottles of cold water.

Perfect for this hot day!

The group's concern and style attracted a crowd of fifty to sixty people. After my son and I drank up our cool refreshment, our physical thirst was satisfied.

I called this group Sarah Satisfaction.

Moments later, we were invited to join their fellowship—a non-religious philosophical group holding the view that God and the universe are the same.

Why do you think Sarah Satisfaction drew a crowd?

What need was met?

How was their version of love demonstrated?

Let's return to Bullhorn Billy.

This guy spoke God's truth. We *are* sinners in need of repentance. And, although Bullhorn Billy didn't attract people to his message, he was faithful and obedient to God's command: *Go into all the world and proclaim the gospel to the whole creation* (Mark 15:15).

God must love his committed heart.

But while Bullhorn Billy spoke truth, he left out the hope of the gospel—our free gift.

Conversely, Sarah Satisfaction told lies, yet she drew crowds.

What lesson can we glean from this pagan group?

Two Women Share the Truth

I get giddy when I play the reactions from this scenario in my mind—the resurrection account in Matthew 28:1–10.

Right here. Women and gossip. Best ever.

According to the Gospels, a group of women, including Mary Magdalene and the other Mary, went to the tomb. I love how the angel positioned himself on a rock as if to say, *I want to be first row to witness their grief turn to joy.*

The angel said to the women, "Do not be afraid. I know you seek Jesus. He's risen! Go tell the good news quickly!"

Tell. Spread the word. Yep, best news ever. Good gossip.

Shock or confusion may have accompanied their joy. But they didn't question the angel or insist on proof. The women hustled with joy to Galilee, eager spread the good news. Sure enough, just as the angel had said, they ran into Jesus!

Hmm. I wonder about Jesus's countenance when He saw the women coming toward Him.

I can't help but consider Jesus's delight at watching His beloved friends and disciples be joyful about His resurrection. Can you? Do you think He laughed? I believe Jesus takes pleasure when we talk about Him. I envision the sweetest countenance: Jesus smiles, closes His eyes, and sweetly lowers His head, then gently laughs. Raising his head, eyes twinkling, He summons the angels and points in her direction. She's mine and she's telling others about me!

The entire scenario makes me beam. And cry tears of joy.

People Listen to Good News

Paul hadn't visited Colosse. He had only heard through the grapevine about what the Christians were up to. More good gossip. He writes in Colossians 1:4, *Because we have heard of your faith in Christ Jesus and of the love you have for all God's people.*

In the opening of this Bible study, you heard about God's faithfulness to me. When I needed a college education, God made a way. He equipped me with the skill of sign language to offset tuition.

Best news. Good gossip!

People also listen for hope. I "accidently" shared about the hope we have in Jesus when I was experiencing deep grief:

> It had been a hard morning. I meandered to the community pool
> where I could gather my thoughts. My Bible was open on my lap,
> and I was holding a Bible study guide with my right hand. An
> older woman got out of the pool, grabbed her towel from the chair
> beside me, and started drying off. With swollen eyes still wet from
> tears, I looked her straight in the eye. Despite my sorrow, I smiled.

"It looks like you're studying," she said.

"Yes, I am. Are you familiar with this study?" She glanced down at my Bible and accompanying Bible study book and responded, "Oh no . . . I'm an agnostic." I knew what that meant, but I wanted to hear it from her.

"What does that mean?"

Flinging her hands in the air she said, "Don't know ... don't care."

I was surprised, but I nodded and continued to smile. "Yeah . . . I believe God created me and has a purpose for me. I'm just experiencing some tough stuff right now. I've received bad news, so I'm reading my Bible, searching for hope."

She continued to dry her back but looked deep into my eyes.

"You radiate," she said. "You're the kind of Christian Jesus was talking about."

She knew how Jesus defined Christians?

Jesus shone through the cracks of my brokenness, reflecting a holy presence. A woman who didn't care about His existence admitted, "I see Jesus in you."[131]

When God brings this experience to my mind, I pray for this woman. I believe a seed of hope was planted in this woman who perhaps one day will experience deep grief. Then God will remind her of the day she saw a woman searching for hope in the Bible. She will go look for herself and find Jesus. I often wonder about meeting her again in heaven. Don't be intimidated; share your reality.

Think About Your Story

You may still be unsure about the most effective way to witness. After all, witnessing can be scary, daunting, even intimidating.

Do I share on streetcorners or leave gospel tracks in conspicuous places? Maybe.

What if I mess up? You won't.

I can't remember Scripture, and I don't know the right words. It's okay.

Besides, I'm shy. Lame excuse.

Moses had some of these same concerns. God told him in Exodus 4:12, *Now therefore, go, and I will be with your mouth and teach you what you shall say.*

If the word "witnessing" sounds scary, think of it instead as "sharing your story." It feels less intimidating when thinking of it in this light.

It's like this. You're talking with people about an incident. Like the news. You're telling about something God did. What you're doing is bragging on God!

We don't have to have a gospel tract, a Bible, or even verses memorized (although these are helpful). We can be spontaneous and transparent.

When reflecting on your personal story, consider these questions:

- How did you hear about God?
- Did you grow up believing there was a God or were you hesitant?
- Did you know He was pursuing you?
- Can you recall a specific time when you called out to God?
- Was there a situation you needed help with, and He answered?
- Did trauma or grief build your faith?

On another piece of paper, write down your story. Share how God's faithfulness changed your understanding of Him.

Plan

The Bible tells us in 1 Peter 3:15–16:

> *Always be prepared to give an answer to everyone who asks you to give the reason for the hope that you have. But do this with gentleness and respect, keeping a clear conscience, so that those who speak maliciously against your good behavior in Christ may be ashamed of their slander.*

Take some time to pray and contemplate about your personal gospel conversation opportunities.

On the left side of the box, list potential events or places where you could share your testimony. On the right side of the box, list people that God has placed on your heart to talk with.

Places or Events	People

Planning ahead of time can relieve stressful anxiety to anxious excitement!

Pray

If you still need courage—all of us do—use the following verses as your prayers:

- *Now, Lord, look on their threats, and grant to Your servants that with all boldness they may speak Your word.* (Acts 4:29)

- *Whenever I am afraid, I will trust in You.* (Psalm 56:3)

- *Do not fear, for I am with you; do not be afraid, for I am your God. I will strengthen you, I will also help you, I will also uphold you with My righteous right hand.* (Isaiah 41:10 NASB)

- *Have I not commanded you? Be strong and courageous! Do not be terrified nor dismayed, for the LORD your God is with you wherever you go.* (Joshua 1:9 NASB)

Share Your Story

Now you're ready for an informal conversation. Here are a few things to consider when having a gospel conversation, especially with unbelievers or those who have a difficult life and/or controversial behaviors:

1. Don't get hung up on theology or religious terminology (often called Christianese). Use simple, common words that are easy to understand. These words share the gospel, too. For example, on the left of the chart are some religious terms. On the right are words most people identify with. And the two columns express the same ideas.

Redeemed	Jesus's death bought us back
Forgiven	Pardoned; excused
Justified	Made right with God, not held accountable for our wrong doing
Reconciled	Brought into a right relationship with Jesus
Sanctified	Lifelong process of becoming more like Jesus

2. Turn what God did for you into what God can do for them. When we talk to others about what God has done in our life, the Holy Spirit begins to work in the hearts of those who hear. Don't worry about how to answer every person's question or their reactions to what you say. Describe what Jesus did for you and the Holy Spirit will do the rest.

3. Explain *why* you have joy. Convey that God is your source of strength. Talk about the peace you have, for example, and where it comes from.

4. Resist disagreeing with their viewpoint in a confrontational way. You don't want to start an argument. Rather, share how God answered your prayer. Shine His light. Continue to point to Him.

5. Don't appear to be shocked at what someone shares with you. They could interpret your reaction as judgmental.

6.   If possible, stay in communication with the person with whom you are sharing. Pray for them as God brings them to mind.

The Bible tells a story of a healed blinded man who said, "I believe, Lord" (John 9:38).

You believe because God's faithfulness is evident in your life. Share your story, and others will believe as well.

Our journey through this Bible study comes to a close. But as long as we're talking about Jesus and believing His words, we'll continue to be victorious together. And we're promised in Matthew 13:43, *Then the righteous will shine forth as the sun in the kingdom of their Father. He who has ears to hear, let him hear!*

Let's shine together, forever!

Day One's Sparkling Gem: I believe my story shines His light.

Prayer: Father, Thank You for giving me a story. Give me courage to share it. In Jesus's name, amen.

Perspective: Keep writing your story. Keep shining the Light.

Appendix A

How to Make a Decision for Jesus

The most important decision you will ever make has nothing to do with other people or anything on this earth. It doesn't even have anything to do with organized religion or a specific denomination.

The most important decision you'll ever make is whether to have a personal relationship with Jesus Christ. This decision brings peace because you'll know you will spend eternity in heaven with God.

God's way is simple. We don't have to clean up our lives. We come to God as we are, and He cleans us up.

God is holy and cannot look upon sin. So out of His great love, compassion, and mercy for all of humanity, God made a way for us to be in right relationship with Him. He sent His Son, Jesus, to be the sacrifice and die on a cross for us. John 3:16 tells us, *God so loved the world that He gave His only Son that whosoever believes in Him will not perish but have everlasting life.*

Admit you are a sinner—a person who sins. Ask God's forgiveness. Believe Jesus died on the cross and three days later rose from death to life. Ask Him to be your Savior and take control of your life.

God has a beautiful plan and purpose for you. You may find it easier to use this prayer:

> God, I know I'm a sinner. I'm sorry for my sins, and I ask Your forgiveness. I believe You sent Your Son, Jesus Christ, as a sacrifice and He died and rose again. I invite You into my life. I give You control. Thank You for saving me. I know I will spend eternity with You. In Jesus's name, amen.

If you prayed this prayer, welcome to the family of God!

Please let someone know. You can email me at debpres@yahoo.com. Attend a Bible-believing church and cultivate this new, amazing relationship with God.

Group Leader Discussion Questions

Week One:

What stood out to you this week?

Describe yourself positively to your group. What specific abilities did God give you?

When do you feel most cherished by God?

What, if anything, makes it difficult to believe that you are God's masterpiece?

How does knowledge of "God's seal on you" empower you?

What area are you most vulnerable to Satan's attacks?

What specifically do you do to suit up for battle each day? Are you fearful about stopping something or starting something?

What do you need courage to accomplish?

Why is it essential to release our independence?

Week Two:

What stood out to you this week?

Which scripture is most meaningful to you to help you replace negative thoughts with positive ones?

How is your heart like Mary's? Martha's?

What is your reaction to the virtuous woman in Proverbs 31?

What character trait is one of your most beautiful fragrances?

When did someone's words encourage you? Hurt you?

Week Three:

What stood out to you this week?

What attributes of God have impacted you recently?

Which area of wisdom impacted you the most?

Are you comfortable with confrontation or would you rather avoid it?

Esther and Abigail both discerned God's will and acted. In what ways are you like them? How are you different?

Which spiritual fruit is easier to naturally demonstrate? Which one(s) is a challenge?

How did God amaze you this week?

Week Four:

What stood out to you this week?

Are you in the fires now or coming out?

How do you stay anchored, especially in a trial?

What brings you joy?

What causes you to disconnect from the Vine?

How do you connect or reconnect?

When is it difficult to stay faithful to God? What keeps you faithful?

Week Five:

What stood out to you this week?

What has God put on your heart to build?

What needs to be torn down?

What is broken in your sphere of influence?

What battle are you facing?

What's your battle plan?

Is prayer easy for you? Why or why not?

What legacy is unfolding?

Thank you!

I want to express my thanks and gratitude to the women who attended this Bible study so I could practice and get feedback. Your thoughts and ideas were (and are) wonderful!

To my Enrich Café Critique Group, your suggestions and help were significant. I will always be grateful.

To my best friends who have not only walked with me throughout life, but also stuck with me through this study as I labored, I thank you for your prayers and the times you made me rest and checked on my health. I love our walks and talks. I adore you.

To my Fab Four group, everyone needs a group of godly women for support, prayer, and accountability. And fun! Did I mention, fun? I am thankful I have you!

Denise, thank you for your expert editing services. You make my words shine a bit brighter. Meg, I thank you friend for your excellent videography. You helped make my dream and vision a reality.

Thank you, Kim, for walking me through the publishing process and helping me get this Bible study into the hands of readers. I am so thankful!

Mostly … and forever … I thank you, Precious Lord. You are my Father and Savior. But these last few years, I have experienced you more than ever as my very best friend.

Alan. My precious Alan. I will always love you.

To the women participating in this Bible study,
thank you for choosing mine.
I love you.

About the Author

Debbie Presnell's career has spanned four decades of teaching—from elementary school to higher education, where she trained future teachers. She is a member of Gardner-Webb University's Gallery of Distinguished Alumni, a published author, national speaker, and Bible study teacher. She is also the United States spokesperson for Mukti Mission in India where she partners with Mukti Mission US to bring hope, healing, and life to women and children of India.

Debbie has authored five books:

- *Shine! Radiating the Love of God—A Bible Study Designed for Young Women in Middle School and High School*
- *Shining Through the Psalms—A 150- Day Devotional Journey*
- *Shine On! 30 Biblical Principles for Radiant Living*
- *Shining Through James—Living the Journey that Doesn't Make Sense*
- *Believing God's Perspective, Design, and Purpose for Women, A Six-Week Bible Study Based on Psalm 144:12*

Additionally, her articles have been published in the *Divine Moments* series and on *Crosswalk.com*. She is a member of *Advanced Writers and Speakers Association* (AWSA).

Debbie is founder and president of *Shine Camp and Conferences, Inc.*, a 501c(3) non-profit organization, whose mission is to use biblical principles to encourage women of all ages to embrace their identity in Christ, fulfill their purpose, impact the community, and shine!

Debbie and her late husband have three adult children, two sons-in-love, and three grandchildren. She enjoys hiking and riding her bike. She loves both the mountains and the beach and spending time with her family.

For more information about Shine Camp for teen girls, weekend Shine Conferences for moms, daughters, and grandmothers, or Debbie's speaking ministry to women, visit her website at www.debbiepresnell.com. Connect with her on Facebook, Instagram, and YouTube: Shine Every Day With Debbie. Email her at debbie@debbiepresnell.com.

Endnotes

1. christiancourier.com/articles/305-lord-and-lord-whats-the-difference

2. https://www.christianity.com/bible/kjv/psalm/144-12-15#f1

3. ibid

4. *Merriam-Webster's Online Dictionary*, Copyright 2015 by Merriam Webster, Incorporated

5. biblestudytools.com/commentaries/treasury-of-david/psalms-144-12.html

6. Deborah Presnell, *Shining Through the Psalms*, Grace Publishing, 2018, 155-156.

7. Susan Hunt, *Spiritual Mothering: The Titus 2 Model for Women Mentoring Women*, https://www.goodreads.com/book/show/354980.Spiritual_Mothering.

8. https://bukrate.com/author/priscilla-shirer-quotes?p=4

9. https://www.merriam-webster.com/dictionary/atonement

10. https://www.npr.org/sections/krulwich/2012/09/17/161096233/which-is-greater-the-number-of-sand-grains-on-earth-or-stars-in-the-sky

11. https://www.crosswalk.com/faith/spiritual-life/inspiring-quotes/40-powerful-quotes-from-corrie-ten-boom.html

12. dictionary.com/browse/adopt

13. https://www.ibelieve.com/faith/30-inspirational-quotes-from-beth-moore.html

14. https://www.merriam-webster.com/dictionary/liar

15. https://www.biblegateway.com/passage/?search=Mark+12%3A41-44&version=NKJV

16. https://www.brainyquote.com/quotes/dwight_l_moody_

17. https://quotefancy.com/joni-eareckson-tada-quotes

18. https://www.seeker.com/when-asked-once-if-he-was-afraid-of-anything-thomas-edison-replied-i-a-1819488636.html

19. https://www.merriam-webster.com/dictionary/fast

20. https://www.dictionary.com/e/fasting/

21. https://www.biblestudytools.com/dictionaries/bakers-evangelical-dictionary/fast-fasting.html

22. https://twitter.com/jdgreear/status/580708246719242240?lang=en

23. https://allauthor.com/quotes/63985/

24. https://biblehub.com/hebrew/6662.htm

25. https://biblehub.com/greek/1342.htm

26. https://biblehub.com/greek/5046.htm

27. Warren W. Wiersbe, *Be Worshipful,* David C. Cook, 2009, 66.

28. ailymail.co.uk/femail/article-3029777/Dove-survey-reveals-96-CENTwomen-rate-average- looking.html

29. https://www.biblestudytools.com/dictionary/myrrh/

30. https://www.atthewellproject.com/blog//8-benefits-of-myrrh-oil-beauty-secrets-in-the-bible

31. https://biblehub.com/hebrew/4753.htm

32. https://www.christianity.com/bible/commentary/spur/psalm/45

33. https://quoteinvestigator.com/author/garson/page/160/

34. https://kidadl.com/quotes/best-a-beautiful-mind-quotes-to-inspire-you

35. https://odb.org/US/2020/08/23/no-fishing-allowed

36. https://www.biblestudytools.com/lexicons/greek/kjv/phroneo.html

37. https://www.studylight.org/commentaries/eng/bnb/2-timothy-1.html

38. http://christian-quotes.ochristian.com/Beauty-Quotes/

39. Deborah Presnell, *Shining Through the Psalms*. Grace Publishing, 2018. 107.

40. biblehub.com/Luke/10-41.htm- Gill's Exposition & Elliott's commentary

41. *The NKJV Personal Study Bible,* Thomas Nelson, 1549, Focus Notes for Pharisee and Scribe.

42. biblehub.com/Greek/3759.htm, meaning of woe.

43. https://www.dictionary.com/browse/contrite

44. http://christian-quotes.ochristian.com/Beauty-Quotes/page-3.shtml

45. https://www.merriam-webster.com/dictionary/majesty

46. https://biblehub.com/hebrew/1935.htm

47. https://www.merriam-webster.com/dictionary/

48. https://www.gotquestions.org/tear-clothes-Bible.html

49. https://www.bibletools.org/index.cfm/fuseaction/Lexicon.show/ID /G2885/kosmeo.htm

50. https://www.azquotes.com/quotes/topics/smell.html

51. https://www.ranker.com/list/best-smells/jacob-shelton

52. https://www.merriam-webster.com/dictionary/meal%20offering

53. https://www.azquotes.com/author/14530-Mother_Teresa/

54. https://travelmelodies.com/beautiful-words/

55. *Merriam-Webster's Online Dictionary*, copyright © 2015 by Merriam-Webster, Incorporated/abusive; foul

56. https://www.christianity.com/bible/commentary/matthew-henry-complete/psalm/144

57. https://biblehub.com/commentaries/proverbs/9-1.htm

58. https://biblehub.com/commentaries/proverbs/9-1.htm

59. https://www.vocabulary.com/dictionary/hewn

60. https://quotefancy.com/quote

61. https://www.chapman.edu/wilkinson/research-centers

62. https://www.verywellmind.com/list-of-phobias-2795453

63. https://utmost.org/quotes/2331/

64. https://kingjamesbibledictionary.com/StrongsNo/H3372/fear

65. https://www.google.com/search?q=strongs+meaning+for+yirah

66. https://www.biblestudytools.com/lexicons/hebrew/kjv/chanan.html

67. https://biblehub.com/greek/2285.htm

68. https://www.brainyquote.com/quotes/charles_spurgeon

69. https://www.inspiringquotes.us/author/4445-henry-blackaby

70. thefreedictionary.com/wisdom and knowledge

71. biblehub.com/greek/4678.htmWisdom- Greek word sophias

72. Warren W. Wiersbe, *Be Mature*, David C. Cook, 2008, 111

73. https://studiojakemedia.com/2022/04/24/vance-havner-god-uses-broken-things

74. biblehub.com/commentaries/2_timothy/4-2.htm

75. gospelhall.org/bible/bible.php?passage=2%20Timothy+4&ver1=kjv&commentary=jamison

76. vocabulary.com dictionary

77. biblestudytools.com/lexicons/greek/nas/parakaleo.htm

78. https://theriverbendgroup.com/considering-the-difference-between-right-and-almost-right

79. https://dictionary.cambridge.org/us/dictionary/english/discern

80. https://www.vocabulary.com/dictionary/discernment

81. https://faithgateway.com/products/the-fruit-of-the-spirit-becoming-the-person-god-wants-you-to-be

82. Deborah Presnell, *Shining Through the Psalms,* Grace Publishing, 2018, 52.

83. Wiersbe, *Be Mature* (David C. Cook, 2008), 115-119.

84. Albert Barnes, *Albert Barnes' NT Commentary*, quoted in Larry Pierce, *The Online Bible*, CD-ROM (Winterbourne, Ontario: Larry Pierce, 2007), Psalm 144:12.

85. Matthew Poole, *Matthew Poole's Commentary*, quoted in Phil Lindner, *Power Bible CD*, CD-ROM (Bronson, Mich.: Online Publishing, Inc., 2007), Psalm 144:12.

86. Thomas Scott, *Thomas Scott Commentary*, quoted in Phil Lindner, *Power Bible CD*, CD-ROM (Bronson, Mich.: Online Publishing, 2007), Psalm 144:12.

87. Charles Spurgeon, *Treasury of David*, quoted in Phil Lindner, *Power Bible CD*, CD-ROM (Bronson, Mich.: Online Publishing, Inc., 2007), Psalm 144:12.

88. https://www.merriam-webster.com/dictionary/polished

89. https://biblehub.com/greek/5046.htm

90. biblestudytools.com/lexicons/greek/nas/purosis.html

91. biblehub.com/greek/3986.htm-Peirasmos

92. biblehub.com/greek/1383.htm-Dokimion

93. https://www.google.com/search?q=what+does+vitality+mean+in+collins+dictionary

94. https://www.goodreads.com/quotes/255850-of-one-thing-i-am-perfectly-sure-god-s-story-never

95. *New King James Version, Personal Study Bible* (Nashville: Nelson Publishing, 1995)

96. https://www.azquotes.com/quote/809533

97. https://www.collinsdictionary.com/us/dictionary/english/mire

98. https://www.goodreads.com/quotes/43372-hope-itself-is-like-a-star--not-to-be-seen

99. https://www.merriam-webster.com/dictionary/abound

100. https://ajoyfueledjourney.com/64-powerful-christian-quotes/

101. *New King James Version, Personal Study Bible* (Nashville: Nelson Publishing, 1995)

102. https://utmost.org/classic/is-your-hope-in-god-faint-and-dying-classic/

103. Wiersbe, *Be Mature* (Colorado Springs: David C. Cook, 2008) 115-119

104. https://www.facebook.com/InTouchMinistries/photos/

105. *New King James Version, Personal Study Bible* (Nashville: Nelson Publishing, 1995)

106. https://www.christianity.com/bible/commentary/matthew-henry-complete/psalm/144

107. https://www.dictionary.com/browse/venerable

108. https://www.google.com/search?q=cornerstone

109. https://namesforgod.net/cornerstone/?cn-reloaded=1

110. https://www.crosswalk.com/faith/spiritual-life/inspiring-quotes/40-inspiring-quotes-from-elisabeth-elliot.html

111. https://www.goodreads.com/quotes/7474411

112. https://quotefancy.com/quote/1477202/Philip-Yancey-

113. https://www.usnews.com/news/health-news/articles/2022-09-19/depression-affects-almost-1-in-10-americans

114. https://clubhouse-intl.org/our-impact/about-mental-illness/

115. https://worldpopulationreview.com/state-rankings/divorce-rate-by-state

116. https://www.tfah.org/report-details/pain-in-the-nation-2022/

117. https://www.biblestudytools.com/commentaries/matthew-henry-complete/ezekiel/13.html

118. https://livehim.com/10-inspiring-quotes-from-christian-leaders/

119. https://www.cnbc.com/2021/03/10/more-than-half-of-us-women-are-burned-out-heres-how-to-cope.html

120. Webster's Online

121. https://www.joniandfriends.org/be-still/

122. https://www.pewresearch.org/religion/religious-landscape-study/frequency-of-prayer/

123. "Vigilant." *Merriam-Webster.com Dictionary,* Merriam-Webster, https://www.merriam-webster.com/dictionary/vigilant. Accessed 28 Jan. 2023.

124. Deborah Presnell, *Shine On: 30 Biblical Principles for Radiant Living.* Grace Publishing, 2020.

125. https://www.brainyquote.com/quotes/billy_graham_626354

126. https://www.oxfordlearnersdictionaries.com/us/definition/american_english/legacy_1

127. https://gracequotes.org/author-quote/james-moffatt/

128. https://www.goodreads.com/work/quotes/48857599-the-magnolia-story?page=4

129. biblestudytools.com/dictionary/sanctification

130. https://www.goodreads.com/quotes/

131. Deborah Presnell, *Shining Through the Psalms,* Grace Publishing, 2018, 73.